François de Salignac de La Mothe- Fénelon

Three Dialogues on Pulpit Eloquence

François de Salignac de La Mothe- Fénelon
Three Dialogues on Pulpit Eloquence
ISBN/EAN: 9783744660488
Printed in Europe, USA, Canada, Australia, Japan
Cover: Foto ©Lupo / pixelio.de

More available books at **www.hansebooks.com**

THREE DIALOGUES
ON
PULPIT ELOQUENCE.

THREE DIALOGUES

ON

PULPIT ELOQUENCE

BY

Mgr. FRANÇOIS de SALIGNAC de LAMOTHE FÉNÉLON

Archbishop of Cambray

TRANSLATED

AND

ILLUSTRATED BY QUOTATIONS FROM MODERN WRITERS

WITH AN

INTRODUCTORY ESSAY

BY THE LATE

SAMUEL J. EALES, M.A., D.C.L.,

Vicar of Stalisfield, Kent,

EDITOR AND TRANSLATOR OF THE WORKS OF S. BERNARD;
OF BISHOP DUPANLOUP'S "MINISTRY OF PREACHING," ETC.

LONDON: PHILADELPHIA:

THOMAS BAKER.   JOHN McVEY.

1897.

Introductory Essay.

A GREAT French Bishop, who has not long since passed away, Mgr. Félix Dupanloup, of Orleans, speaks thus of the object set before the Christian Preacher: "Men who undertake the ministry of the Word in a serious manner do not speak in the pulpit for the mere sake of speaking, but to teach, to convert, and to save souls." That is a function which has been needful in some form in every age of human history ever since the Fall, and it is tolerably sure to continue needful to the end. There have been ministries even in the Church of Christ which have had, as time went on, to be altered in form, or even dropped altogether, because of the change in the outward circumstances of the Church, or in the minds of men (1 *Cor.* xii. 7-10, 28). No such change is likely seriously to affect the ordinance of Preaching, and that for two reasons: first, because it is based on a fundamental fact in human nature, which cannot in any stage of civilization, be got rid of, *i.e.: the influence of one human soul upon other human souls;* and next, because it employs that principle in the very simplest form possible. There are many other and more highly specialized forms of it—the drama, the orchestra, the poem, and indeed, literature in general, especially the daily and weekly press. But each of these, it will be found, either limits its own aim or is limited by its necessary conditions. The *drama*, as presented in some crowded and brilliantly-lighted theatre, bends all the resources of art to create *illusion*. The audience is carried away to the mimic spectacle presented on the stage, and is absorbed for the moment in the personality presented before them of Hamlet or of Lear, of the "dainty Ariel" or the impassioned Juliet.

There is an illusion in the power of music, though it does indeed

> "take the prison'd soul
> And lap it in Elysium."

But what a mass of long and patient training in the performers, of costly and elaborate appliances of a highly scientific kind in the instruments does a powerful orchestra or band present! To a great musical performance, as to a drama fully rendered, belong, therefore, the expenditure of large pecuniary means, and of the efforts of many highly-trained and gifted performers; and the use of those great and important agencies, as a whole, is accordingly limited to the places and the occasions where and when those indispensable auxiliaries can be commanded.

Literature, again, and particularly that form of it with which we are so familiar, as the daily, weekly, or periodical press, differs from oratory in some degree as to its *functions*. It is the intellect which its conductors and its writers have principally to address. Their object is to inform, to delight, or to instruct. The calm perusal of a book occupies the mind, rather than arouses the feelings. It produces, perhaps, a more lasting effect than an impassioned address from a living voice; but does not make so powerful an impression at the time. Besides, the voice of the speaker is far more *popular*. Not all *can* read; not all who can have the leisure to read; while lastly, not all who have the ability and the leisure to read, are willing to do so. But all are capable of being approached and influenced through the ear, and by the living voice of an earnest speaker. No elaborate apparatus or lengthy training of musical performers, no dramatic illusion, laboriously prepared by the aid of all the arts are needful for this. The means are the simplest imaginable; or rather it should be said that no means whatever are necessary for oratory to produce its fullest effect. On the one side the auditory; on the other the single voice of the speaker or preacher. That is all that is required for eloquence to "do its perfect work," and to establish over the hearts and wills of those subjected to its power, a dominion which, if it be more or less transitory and passing, is complete and perfect while it lasts.

It need not, therefore, be much feared that the orator, upon things secular, or the preacher, of things spiritual, will speedily find his "occupation gone," and himself deemed superfluous even in these times of daily newspapers and multitudinous literature; always provided that the speaker or the preacher rise to the level of the occasion set before him, and be himself, in all points, equal to his task.

That leads us a step further to consider what is the task set before the preacher, and what does it require of him in order to its fulfilment more or less completely. Now S. Paul, when instructing Timothy, who was probably one of the earliest preachers of the Word, lays down the object of preaching to be "*godly edifying which is in faith*" (1 *Tim.* i. 4); and in a second reference to the subject, he bids Timothy "*reprove, rebuke, and exhort*" (2 *Tim.* iv. 2). The preacher is, indeed, to teach; but, in our own day especially, there are other agencies for teaching, and these are in some respects more effective than the pulpit. To read to a congregation a calm and reasoned essay, even upon some religious subject, is to trespass upon the territory of literature. A book that is under the eye, that can be read and reread, and slowly gathered, by repeated perusals, into the treasure-house of the mind, is a far more effectual instrument for detailed doctrinal teaching as such, than the ἔπεα πτερόεντα, once heard and fleeting, of the preacher; not to speak of the catechetical class with its teacher, which is a more powerful agency than either for the mere imparting of knowledge. The preacher has to teach, indeed; but, as it were, incidentally. The Church of Christ has no esoteric doctrines held in reserve, to be doled forth from time to time by the lips of its ministers. He has no doctrinal novelties which it is his task to display to his hearers. He has a message to deliver, but it is the old message of the Fathers, the Faith "once delivered unto the Saints." He may not add to it, as he may not diminish aught from it in the delivering; yet he is so to deliver it that it shall come with an altogether new force and power to those who hear it. He has to evoke and call into action the imagination of his hearers by the powerful working of his own spiritual faculties, so that it shall acquire a new vision of the eternal realities; to act upon their memory, that it may bring to light the hidden things of their past experience; and most of all, upon their affections, that gratitude and remorse, and hope and fear may enlist the inert or wavering will upon the side of right, and carry the whole man away from evil, and along the paths of good. In short, it is the preacher's task to present, not religious truths in an abstract, or conventionalized, or uninteresting form; but religious truths *touched with emotion;*—winged with the energy, and power, and the dynamic force of the preacher's own mind and soul, that so they may strike other souls, and impress and influence them powerfully, and finally win them to good.

This is the task set before the preacher; and in the performance, with more or less of adequacy, of this task, lies the true power of the pulpit. It is, we maintain, the chief and most important task; not, of course, the only one. The preacher has to comfort, to warn, to soothe, to build up souls in the Faith; but all in constant remembrance of the primary work given him to do—to proclaim the simple message of salvation to sinful souls. "*These ought ye to have done, and not to leave the other undone.*"

It would seem, then, that if the preaching of the Word be in any case weak and ineffective, it is to the absence from it of this qualification, or the neglect to direct it to this its chief object, that the weakness must be owing. No parish priest ought to be satisfied to deliver addresses to his people, Sunday after Sunday, which produce no apparent effect, and from which to all human perception, no result follows. Can he be said to have fulfilled his duty to his congregation as a preacher of the Word, after the reading to them of a Sermon[*] which has left their consciences and their feelings, their aspirations after good, and their repulsion from evil, wholly unaffected, strictly *in statu quo*, and every pulse beating with its wonted calm? Would S. Paul have been satisfied with such a result at the close of one of his missionary addresses? Does it not seem that in such a Sermon, falling almost unheeded from the pulpit, there must have

---

[*] The late Dr. Döllinger is said to have once observed to Mr. Gladstone: "Depend upon it, if the Church of England is to make way, and be a thoroughly National Church, the Clergy must give up the practice of preaching from written sermons." And not less remarkable is the opinion of Cardinal Newman upon this point: "I think it no extravagance to say that a very inferior sermon delivered without book answers the purpose for which all sermons are delivered, more perfectly than one of great merit if it be written and read."

wanting that vital spark of spiritual life which could not have failed to give it power; and that element which we inferred above to be the especial and peculiar strength and endowment of the preacher,—*religious teaching touched with emotion*. Without this, that is to say, without an earnest love for souls and a conscious energetic effort to bring about their conversion, or their edification, "our exhortation lacks sincerity, and is no more, in truth, than a kind of falsehood, cold and frozen; it is an utterance of the mind, and not of the heart."[*]

The preacher in such a case will have his audience unaffected by what he is saying, because he himself does not feel it deeply enough. The religious emotion, that is to say, cannot be *manufactured;* it must be communicated from him who speaks to those who listen. To make them feel, you must feel yourself. The electric spark that shall make a great audience responsive to your appeals and ready to absorb and assimilate your teachings must first be generated in your own soul. This earnest sincerity of spirit in the preacher, bent upon doing a real work for and upon souls, is what the Fathers call *unction;* and it is that quality in a Sermon which is sure to make it effective for good to some soul and in some manner; while its absence in a Sermon, however learned or however eloquent, condemns that Sermon to be sterile; leaves it no better

---

[*] Bishop Dupanloup.

than husks,—"dry bread," upon which no soul can feed to its edification.

Victor Hugo says in one of his works: "*Les Travailleurs de la Mer*," when describing some nautical machine, that it was full of faults in construction, "*but it moves all the same.*" So we may say of a Sermon which is inspired with this breath of life, with this strong throb of religious emotion and impulse, that, however full of faults it may be, it will, nevertheless, not fail to have its due effect. *It is alive;* and its spiritual energy will wake those who hear it into a corresponding throb of life and feeling. They may recognise faults of various kinds in it: limitations in the spiritual vision of the preacher, imperfections in his delivery of his message; but still, it will appeal to their minds and souls, as in its measure, being a true message from behind the veil—a voice from the unseen, "the telephone of eternity," as it has been said, "speaking in the ear of time." Then further, it is from this central and vital principle that all the splendour and warmth, all the exuberance and enrichment of lofty and powerful oratory may, under favouring circumstances, be born and shoot into luxuriant leafage and bloom. "When the tongue of fire sits upon, or uses as its vehicle, a high intelligence; when large powers are chambers through which celestial lights and fires stream; when language, thought, and imagination are equally and alike enkindled; it surely is not unnatural to expect effects and influences corresponding to the magnificent vocation."*

To promote this sincerity and depth of earnestness, this vital energy and force, this natural and unsophisticated utterance in the performance of the high function of the Christian pulpit, is substantially the object of the following dialogues. They will not, perhaps, be less useful to our generation because they reach that result by a road unfamiliar to us, or because the writer appeals to preachers and to precedents for the most part unknown to all but a few scholars. The essential justness of the views maintained by the author upon the eloquence of the pulpit, will enable the "Dialogues" to be still read with pleasure and profit, though we are far from defending certain prejudices or the bad taste of his time, in which, however, he naturally shared; such as, for instance, in asserting that the Gothic architecture came to us from the Arabs; that the enrichments of it are only "gewgaws"; and that it is far inferior to the Greek orders in simplicity, grandeur, and dignity. It is not upon such subjects that we shall take note of his opinion. But if we regard the "Dialogues" as a whole, and reflect upon the power and accuracy with which the great principles of evangelical preaching are set forth in them, we shall not be inclined to think that Bishop Dupanloup estimated

---

* Rev. E. Paxton Hood.

them too highly when he styled the work "a prodigious achievement, which had not been excelled even by the greatest geniuses"; and declared that they set forth "the unchanging principles of reason and wisdom, the unalterable precepts of nature admirably explained"; and expressed the opinion that "if the precepts of Fénelon, here set forth, had been well understood, they would have long since fixed the character of sacred eloquence among us."

They are here presented for the consideration of the English reader; and it is hoped that the illustrative extracts, taken from a great number of contemporary writers, will have the effect of developing and completing discussions, which are, in some instances, too briefly touched upon by our author, and of supplying various considerations which he may have altogether omitted.

That both the one and the other may be of some use in promoting an increasingly earnest, simple, and effectual preaching of the Gospel of JESUS CHRIST, is the desire and hope of the Translator.

SAMUEL J. EALES.

THREE DIALOGUES ON PULPIT ELOQUENCE.

First Dialogue.

Against the affectations of wit and brilliancy in Sermons. That the object of eloquence is to instruct men and render them better, and that the orator who does not aim at this object is not disinterested.*

A : Good morning, sir! have you then been to hear one of the sermons to which you have so often been desirous to take me? For my part, I am contented with the preacher of our parish.

B : I was charmed with mine; you have lost much, sir, by not having been present to hear him. I have rented a seat, so as not to lose one of the sermons for Lent. He is an admirable preacher, if you had once heard him you would be dissatisfied with every other.

A : I shall be careful, then, not to hear him, for I do not at all wish that one preacher should give me a distaste for all others; on the contrary, I wish for a man who will give me such a taste for and

---

* The parties to the Dialogue are designated as A, B, and C.

delight in the Word of God, that I shall be the more disposed to listen to it whenever I can. But since I have, as you say, lost so much by not hearing this fine sermon, and you are full of it, you can make up to me for part of that loss, if you will be so kind as to repeat to me something of what you remember of it.

B: My account would do injustice to the sermon. There were a hundred beauties in it which I fail to remember. It would require a preacher to give you an account . . . .

A: But still; his plan, his demonstrations, his practical lessons, the chief truths which made up the body of his discourse—do none of these remain in your mind? or were you not attentive?

B: Far from it! I never listened with more attention and pleasure.

A: What then! do you wish me to beg and intreat you?

B: No, but there are thoughts so delicate and so dependent on the beauty and turn of the phrase in which they are expressed, that though you are charmed for the moment you cannot easily recall them afterwards, and even if you do recall them, and repeat them in other terms, they lose their force and their beauty, and seem to be no longer the same thoughts.

A: They must then be very fragile beauties indeed if you try to touch them they disappear. I should prefer a discourse which had more substance and less spirit. It would make a stronger impression and would be better remembered. Why does the preacher speak at all if not to instruct and persuade, and to do so in such a fashion that the hearer can remember?

B: Listen, then! I will repeat to you what I am able to remember. This was the text: "I have eaten ashes as it were bread" (Ps. cii. 9). How could you find a more ingenious text for Ash Wednesday? He showed how, according to this passage, ashes ought to be on this day the food of our souls; then he interwove in his introduction, in the most ingenious way in the world, the story of Artemisia and the ashes of her husband. His transition to the "Ave Maria"* was full of art. Then his division of his subject was happy; you shall judge of it. "These ashes," he said,

---

* It was customary at that time, in France, for preachers to introduce into the exordium of their sermons an invocation of the Blessed Virgin and the "Ave Maria"; and great ingenuity was frequently shown in the introduction of this into the special subject of the sermon, such as is remarked upon in the text. Thus L'Esprit Fléchier, Bishop of Lavaur and afterwards of Nimes, who was regarded as one of the chief pulpit orators of France, in his panegyric on S. Joseph, effects this introduction thus: "Everything seems to concur to the glory of my subject; in it the Holy Spirit, Jesus Christ, and Mary, have each an interest. I may then hope for the assistance of the first, the grace of the second, the intercession of the third, that is, the Virgin, to whom we will address ourselves in those words with which the Angel Gabriel addressed himself to her, and which S. Joseph no doubt often recalled and repeated: 'Hail, Mary, etc.'"—*Panegyriques*, Vol. I., p. 71.

"although they are a sign of penitence, are a principle of happiness: although they seem to humble us they are, in reality, a source of glory: although an emblem of death they are a remedy which leads to immortality. This division he repeated in various forms, and each time gave it a new lustre by his antitheses. The rest of the discourse was no less polished and brilliant. The diction was pure, the thoughts novel, the periods harmonious, and each concluded with some surprising touch. He drew sketches of morality, in which each recognized his own likeness faithfully drawn, and anatomized the passions of the human heart in a manner which equalled the Maxims of M. de la Rochefoucault. In short, according to my opinion, it was a masterpiece. And now what do you think of it?

A: I am rather afraid to tell you my opinion of that sermon, or to lower the high estimate which you have of it. We ought to feel respect for the Word of God, to profit by the truths which are explained by a preacher, and to avoid the spirit of criticism, so as not to weaken the authority of the ministry.

B: Do not be afraid of that in the present instance. It is not at all from curiosity that I ask this of you. I have need to have correct ideas upon this matter. I wish to obtain solid information, not only for my own sake, but for that of others, since I too am, by my profession, under the obligation to preach. Speak to me, then, without reserve; do not hesitate to contradict me, nor fear that I shall be shocked.

A : As you wish it I will do so, and even from your report of that sermon I judge that it was exceedingly faulty.

B : In what respect?

A : You will see. Can a sermon be considered good in which the applications of Scripture are false, in which a story out of secular history is related in a puerile and unedifying manner, in which a false affectation of brilliancy is predominant everywhere?

B : Doubtless it cannot, but the sermon of which I have been telling you does not seem to me to be at all of that character.

A : Wait a little, and you will agree with what I say. When a preacher has chosen for his text these words, "I have eaten ashes as it were bread," ought he to have contented himself with tracing out a mere connection of words between the text and the ceremony of this day? Ought he not to have begun by explaining the true sense of his text before applying himself to his subject?

B : No doubt.

A : Would it not also have been desirable to look thoroughly into the circumstances and take the trouble to understand the whole occasion and design of the Psalm? Would it not have been proper to examine if the interpretation about which he was occupied was in accordance with the true sense of the words before giving it to the people as the Word of God?

B: Most truly; but in what respect was it otherwise?

A: David, or whoever was the author of Ps. cii., is speaking in that passage of his own misfortune. He says that his enemies cruelly taunted him, seeing him beaten down into the dust, lying at their feet, and reduced (he uses here a poetical metaphor) to feed upon bread made of ashes, and water mixed with tears. What resemblance is there between the complaints of David, when he was driven from his throne and persecuted by his son Absalom, and the humiliation of a Christian who puts ashes upon his head in order to bring himself to think of death, and to withdraw from the pleasures of the world?* Was there no other text in the Scripture that he could have taken? Had Jesus Christ, the Apostles, the Prophets never spoken of death and

---

* "The allegorical principles of interpretation applied to the Scriptures by Origen and others after him destroyed the legitimate force of the custom of using texts. It destroyed logical connection between text and homily. A text which is torn from its connections in inspired usage, or to which an imaginary sense is given, is no text. This was largely true of the use of texts in the time of Augustine."

—AUSTIN PHELPS, D.D.

of the ashes of the tomb to which God brings down our human weakness? Are not the Scriptures full of a thousand touching phrases about this truth? Would not, for example, the words from Genesis iii. 19, which have been chosen by the Church herself, fitting and natural for this ceremony as they are, would they not have been worthy of a preacher's choice? Had he the false delicacy to find some fault with the text that the Holy Spirit and the Church had desired should be repeated without omission every year? Why, then, should he have put aside that passage and so many other passages of the Scripture which are suitable in order to select one which is not suitable? That is bad taste; a foolish liking for saying something novel.*

B: You are growing too warm on this subject, sir. It is true, however, that this text is not used in a literal sense, but the preacher's explication of it may, nevertheless, have been very fine.

A: For my part I like to know if a saying be

---

* "The reverence for philosophy also weakened the clerical reverence for texts of the Scriptures. In many instances it was deemed a matter of indifference whether texts were chosen from inspired sources or not. Melancthon says that they were sometimes taken from the ethics of Aristotle. This was perfectly natural. A forced interpretation of inspired language brings it into conflict with the common sense of men. In such a conflict no language can hold its place in the reverence of the human mind. When it had become the usage of the pulpit to employ a biblical text as no other language would be seriously employed by a sane mind, it was an improvement to turn from S. Paul to Aristotle, whose language had not yet undergone distortion."—A. PHELPS, D.D.

true before I find any beauty in it. But what as to the remainder?

C. The remainder of the sermon was of the same kind as the text. But what was the advantage of saying pretty things upon a subject so terrible, and of amusing the hearer by the secular story of the grief of Artemisia, when he was bound to speak gravely and solemnly, and to give only terrible ideas of death?

B: I see that you do not love flashes of wit on such occasions. But unless these are allowed, what would become of eloquence? Would you reduce all preachers to the simplicity of Missionaries? That is needful for the unlearned people of course, but those who are cultivated have more delicate ears, and it is necessary to adapt our discourses to their taste.

A: Now you are leading me to another subject, but I was endeavouring to show you how ill-conceived this sermon was, and I was just about to speak of the division of it, but I think that you understand what it is that I am obliged to disapprove of. Here is a man who divides the whole subject of his discourse into three points. Now, when a division is made, it ought to be simple and natural; it should be a division which is found ready made in the subject itself, which clears up the details and arranges them in order, which is itself easily remembered, and which helps the hearer to remember other things: finally, a division which displays the greatness of a subject and of its parts.* But here, on the contrary, you see a man who endeavours in the first place to dazzle you, who displays before you three epigrams, or three riddles, which he turns round and round with a practised hand until you think you are looking at the passes of a juggler. Is that such a serious and grave manner of address as is calculated to make you hope for something useful and important? But let us return to what you were saying: you ask, do I wish them to banish eloquence from the pulpit?

B: Yes, it seems to me that you are tending in that direction.

A: We shall see. What do you understand by eloquence?

B: The art of speaking well.

A: Has that art no other object whatever than

---

* " Divisions thus clearly formed and distinctly stated : (1) Promote perspicuity of discussion. They aid a preacher in gaining perspicuity; clear mental action works instinctively by plan, and each assists the other. You understand a subject the better for having reduced it to a plan of discourse. A natural division of a subject for use is no more nor less than a philosophical analysis and arrangement of its materials; your own thoughts are the more lucid for the discipline. Divisions also assist the hearer to clearness in understanding a discussion. (2) Divisions promote unity of discussion. That preacher must habitually think in slipshod gait who can deliberately plan a vagrant discourse. The very effort to classify materials tends to unify them in the result. (3) They promote progress in a discussion. (4) They promote elegance of discussion, and keep up interest in it, etc."—A. PHELPS, D.D.

that of speaking well? Have men no object whatever in their speech? or do they speak only for the sake of speaking?

B: No! they speak in order to please and to persuade others.

A: Let us carefully distinguish between these two things. The object of speech is to persuade, that is the case always; another object of speech is to please, and this is the case only too often. But when anyone strives to please, he has some other and more distant object, which is nevertheless the principal one. The man of high principle will not seek to please for any other reason than to instil righteousness and other virtues by rendering them attractive, while he who seeks his own interest to increase his reputation or to advance his fortunes, seeks to please only that he may gain the admiration and goodwill of those who are able to satisfy his avarice or his ambition, so that this also comes to be virtually a method of persuasion sought for by the orator: he wishes to please that he may flatter, and thus persuade others to whatever suits his own interest.

B: In short, you cannot but own that men frequently speak only for the purpose of pleasing. Heathen orators had that object. It is easy to discern in the orations of Cicero that he was striving for the sake of his reputation, and who will not believe the same of Isocrates and

Demosthenes? All the ancient panegyrists thought less of making the heroes who were their subjects admired than of being admired themselves: they did not strive to advance the glory of a prince except for the sake of that admiration which would accrue to themselves for having praised him with skill. That ambition seems to have been permitted at all times among both the Greeks and the Romans: by the emulation which resulted, eloquence was rendered perfect, the minds of orators were raised to lofty thoughts and great sentiments, and thus the ancient commonwealths were made to flourish: the intellectual enjoyment which eloquence afforded, and the power which it exercised over the populations, rendered it honourable, and it supplied a marvellously effective means of culture and polish for the intellectual powers. I do not see any reason for blaming that emulation, even among Christian orators, provided that no unbecoming affectation appears in their discourses, and that the morality of the Gospel is not weakened in the least degree. A practice can hardly be blamed which animates young men, and helps to form great preachers.

A : You are grouping together here a great number of facts and reasons: let us separate them if you please, and let us examine attentively what conclusions ought to be drawn from them. But let us especially avoid a contentious spirit: let us look at the matter peaceably, and as people who fear only to be in error: and let us make it a point of honour to give up a position as soon as we see that we are mistaken.

B: I am quite disposed to do this, or at least I think so, and I shall be glad if you will warn me if you see that I am transgressing that rule.

A: Let us not speak of preachers at first; they will come in their turn: let us begin with the secular orators, whose example you have just referred to. You have mentioned Demosthenes and Isocrates together; in that you have done wrong to the former; the second is an orator without warmth or earnestness, whose only care is to polish his sentences and give a harmonious cadence to his periods: his idea of eloquence is not an elevated one, and he makes it to consist almost wholly in the skilful arrangement of words. A man who occupied ten years, as some say, and even twelve according to others, in adjusting the periods of his "Panegyric," which is a discourse on the necessities of Greece, was but a weak and backward helper for the Republic against the enterprises of the King of Persia. Demosthenes spoke against Philip very differently. You may see the comparison which Dionysius of Halicarnassus* makes between the two orators, and the essential defects which he

---

* Died at Rome B.C. 7. The work referred to is Περὶ τῶν ἀρχαίων ῥητόρων ὑπομνηματισμοὶ, and it treated of all the chief orators of Greece. But the second half of the work, sect. 4-6, with the exception of the earlier part of sect. 4, which treats of the oratorical powers of Demosthenes, is not now extant.—*Trans.*

points out in Isocrates. The discourses of the latter he shows to be flowery but feeble, a collection of periods constructed with infinite care to charm the ear: while Demosthenes, on the contrary, influences, warms, and convinces the heart: he is too keenly occupied with the interests of his country to amuse himself, like Isocrates, with sparkling fancies; his reasoning is closely packed and convincing; his sentiments, generous as those of a soul whose conceptions were all noble. His discourse grows and is strengthened at each moment by new reasons, and becomes a chain of striking and impressive figures: you cannot read it without seeing that he has the benefit of his country at heart: it is nature herself that speaks in his impassioned passages; the art is so consummate that it does not appear at all, and nothing has ever equalled the power and vehemence of his orations. Have you never read what Longinus has said of this in his " Treatise on the Sublime "?*

B: No: is it not that treatise which M. Boileau has translated? Is it fine?

A: I do not fear to say that, to my mind, it surpasses the Rhetoric of Aristotle, which, although a very fine treatise, has many dry rules, more curious than useful in practice, so that it is much better adapted to recall the rules of the art to those who are already eloquent, than to inspire eloquence and

---

* Περὶ ὕψους.—*Tr.*

to form a true orator: but the "Sublime" of Longinus adds to its precepts many examples which add greatly to their force. That author treats of the Sublime in a sublime manner, as the translator has remarked: he warms the imagination and elevates the spirit of the reader, forms his taste, and teaches him to distinguish judiciously between what is admirable and what is faulty in the celebrated orations of antiquity.

B: What! is Longinus so admirable! Did he not live in the time of the Emperor Aurelian of Zenobia?

A: Yes; you know their history.

B: Was not that age far below those which preceded it in culture? Would you assert that an author of that period had better taste than Isocrates? I am really unable to believe it.

A: I was myself surprised to find it so, but you have only to read the work to be convinced of the fact. Although it belongs to a debased age it is modelled on earlier models, and has almost nothing of the faults of its time. I say almost nothing, for I must confess that the writer concerns himself more with the ornamental than the useful, and deals but little with the relation between eloquence and morality. In that respect he appears not to have had the same well conceived views as the ancient Greeks, particularly the philosophers. Nevertheless, a defect must be forgiven him in which

Isocrates, although belonging to a better age, is much his inferior; especially that defect is excusable in a passage in which he is professedly speaking, not of that which instructs men, but of that which excites their attention and extorts their admiration. I mention that author, because he will help you much to understand my meaning: you will see in him the admirable portrait which he has drawn of Demosthenes, from whom he quotes, several passages which are truly sublime: and you will find in him also what I have said of the defects of Isocrates. You could make yourself acquainted with those two authors in no better way, if you do not wish to take the trouble to study their works for yourself. Let us then leave Isocrates and return to Demosthenes and to Cicero.

B: You leave Isocrates because his example does not suit your purpose.

A: Let us then discuss him a little more, since you are not yet persuaded: let us judge of his eloquence by the rules of the art itself, and by the opinion of the most eloquent writer of antiquity, that is, Plato; will you believe what he says upon this point?

B: I will believe him if he is right. I do not resign my opinion wholly to the word of any writer.

A: Bear that rule in mind, it grants all that I ask: provided that you do not allow yourself to be biassed by certain prejudices of our time, that which is right and just will soon obtain your assent. Do not, then, believe either Isocrates or Plato, but judge both the one and the other by clearly defined principles. You will not question that the object of eloquence is to persuade the hearers to truth and to virtue.

B: But I do question it; it is that which I have always denied.

A: That, then, is what I am going to prove to you. Eloquence, if I do not mistake, may be taken in three meanings:

(1) As the art of persuading men to accept the truth and of making them better.

(2) As an art of neutral character, of which the wicked may make use as well as the good, and which may be employed to persuade to error and injustice, as well as to justice and truth.

(3) Finally, as an art which designing men may make use of to please others, to acquire reputation for themselves, and to rise to fortune. Now admit one of these definitions.

B: I admit them all; what conclusion can you draw from that?

A: Wait a while; you will see that in the sequel; in the meantime it is sufficient that I say nothing but what is clearly true, and that leads you towards my conclusion. Of these three kinds of eloquence you no doubt approve of the first?

B: Yes, it is the best.

A: And what do you think of the second?

B: I see what you are aiming at; you are going to construct a sophism. The second is blamable for the bad use which the orator permits himself to make of eloquence in order to persuade to injustice and error. Yet the eloquence of a wicked man may be good in itself, though the object for which he makes use of it be pernicious. Well, our present business is to speak of the nature and rules of eloquence, not of the use which ought to be made of it: do not leave, if you please, the real question before us.

A: You will see that I am *not* wandering from it if you will be so good as to do me the favour to continue to listen to me. You blame, then, the second kind of eloquence: and in order to avoid any equivocation, you blame then the second way of employing eloquence.

B: You are quite right, and so far we are fully agreed.

A: And what do you say of the third use of eloquence, which is to endeavour to please the hearers by words, so as to build up by that means a reputation and a fortune?

B: You know already my opinion: I have not changed it in the least. That use of eloquence appears to me allowable and fair: it excites emulation, it polishes talents, and renders them more perfect.

A : In what respect ought it to endeavour to render talents more perfect? If you had to organize a State or a Commonwealth, in what way would you render the abilities of its citizens perfect?

B : In every way which could render them better. I should wish to form good citizens, full of zeal for the public benefit. I should endeavour to ensure that they should be able to defend the country in war, to make the laws observed in peace, to govern their houses, to cultivate their lands or have them cultivated, to bring up their children virtuously, to instil into them a sense of religion, to employ themselves in commerce according to the needs of the country, and to apply themselves to those branches of knowledge which are useful in common life. That is what, it seems to me, should be the aim of a legislator.*

A : Your views are very just and well conceived. You would wish then that your citizens should be enemies to sloth, and be occupied with matters which are serious and which tend to the public good?

B : Yes, doubtless.

A : And you would put down all professions that

---

* "I call, therefore, a complete and generous education that which fits a man to perform justly, liberally and magnanimously all the offices, both private and public, of peace and war."—MILTON, *on Education.*

were not of such a character, that were, in fact, useless?

B: I would.

A: You would not admit, for instance, bodily exercises except such as conduce to health and to strength? I do not make any special mention of bodily symmetry and beauty, because in well-formed frames these follow naturally from strength and health.

B: I should admit such exercises only.

A: You would put down then all those which serve only to amuse, and which do not enable a man to endure better the labours required in peace, and the fatigues of war?

B: Yes, I would follow that rule.

A: And it is, no doubt, in pursuance of the same principle that you would put down also (as you have said to me) all those activities of the mind which do nothing at all to render the soul virtuous, and therefore healthy, beautiful, and strong?

B: Yes; I quite agree to all that, but what follows from it? I do not at all see what is the point you wish to reach; you go so far round about.

A: I am endeavouring to reach first principles, and not to leave behind me any doubtful point. Is all quite clear so far?

B: I must confess that having established this

rule for the body, there seems even stronger reason for applying it to the mind.

A : Would you tolerate all the sciences and the arts whose only object is pleasure, amusement, and the satisfaction of curiosity?

B : I should banish them from my Commonwealth.

A : If, then, you tolerate mathematicians, it would be on account of mechanics, navigation, the surveying of lands, calculations that must be made, fortifications, &c. That is their use, which would entitle them to exist. If you allowed physicians and lawyers it would be for the preservation of health and the ensuring of justice. It would be the same with those other professions which are allowed to be serviceable. But what would you do with regard to musicians? Would you not be of the mind of the ancient Greeks, who never separated that which was useful from that which was agreeable? They who had pushed music and poetry, blended together, to such a high degree of perfection, intended that these should serve to arouse courage and to inspire lofty sentiments. It was by music and poetry that they prepared themselves for battle: they went to war with musicians and their instruments. The drums and trumpets threw them into a kind of warlike transport, which they called Divine. It was by music and the sweet cadence of their verses that they softened the hearts of savage tribes. It was by the pleasure which this harmony occasioned that they introduced wisdom into the hearts of their children. These were made to sing the verses of Homer in order to inspire them, and that in a pleasant manner, with contempt for death, riches, and pleasures which render the mind effeminate; and to inspire also the love of glory, liberty, and of their country. Even their dances had a serious object; for it is certain that they did not dance for pleasure only: we see by the example of David that the Eastern peoples regarded the dance as a serious art, like music or poetry. A thousand words of instruction were mixed with their fables and their poems: and thus the gravest and most austere philosophy showed itself with a smiling face. That appeared again in those mysterious dances of the priests, which heathens had mingled with their ceremonies for the feasts of their gods. All those arts which consist either in melodious sounds, in graceful movements of the body, or in words; that is to say, music, dancing, eloquence and poetry, were invented only to express the passions, and to inspire them by thus expressing. The intention was by means of these to impress lofty sentiments on the minds of men, and to display before them vivid and impressive pictures of the beauty of virtue and the deformity of vice. Thus each of the arts had its place, though under the appearance of pleasure, in the most serious methods of the ancients for the advancement of morality and religion. Even the chase was an apprenticeship for war. All the most enjoyable pleasures were calculated to impart some lesson of virtue. From that source it was that proceeded so many heroic virtues in Greece, which have been the admiration of all ages. That first plan of instruction, it is true, was altered; and even in its original form it had grave defects. Its essential defect was the being grounded on a false and hurtful religion. In that the Greeks, like all the wise men of the world who were at that time sunk in idolatry, fell into error: but though they were in error respecting the fundamentals of religion, and the choice of principles, they made no error as to the right manner of inspiring men with religion and virtue: in that respect their methods were judicious, agreeable, and calculated to make a strong impression.

C: You said just now that this first institution was altered: do not forget, if you please, to explain that to us.

A: Yes, it was altered. Virtue ensures true politeness: but unless care be taken, politeness becomes, little by little, effeminate softness. The Asiatic Greeks were the first to become corrupt; the Ionians* became effeminate; all that coast of Asia was a scene of voluptuous indulgence.† Crete, notwithstanding the wise laws of Minos, was

---

* Motus doceri gaudit Ionicos.—HORACE, B. III., Od. vi., v. 21.
† The Fables of Miletus.

similarly corrupt: you know the verse which S. Paul cites (Tit. i. 12), Corinth was famous for its luxury and its dissoluteness. The Romans, who were still rude and uncultured, were, nevertheless, beginning indulgences tending to soften their rustic virtue. Nor was Athens exempt from that contagion; the whole of Greece was infected. Pleasure, which ought to be only the means of finding an entrance for wisdom, took the place of the wisdom itself. The philosophers protested against this disorder, but in vain. Socrates arose, and pointed out to his misguided fellow citizens that the pleasure, at which they stopped short, ought to be only the road and incentive to virtue. Plato, his disciple, who has not been ashamed to compile his writings from the discourses of his master, excluded from his ideal state (Republic) all the varied tones of music, all the movements of tragedy, all recitations of poems, and even those passages of Homer as do not tend to inculcate a love of good order and wise laws. These are the opinions respecting poets and musicians expressed by Socrates and Plato: are you not in agreement with them?

B: I entirely agree with their opinion: we ought to have nothing that is useless. Since pleasure can be found in important pursuits, it should not be sought elsewhere. If any art can render virtue easier, it is right in that manner to show that virtue is consistent with pleasure: if, on the contrary, they are separated, men are put under strong temptation to abandon virtue: for, after all, that which pleases without instructing, only amuses the mind and renders it effeminate. So you see that I too have become a philosopher merely from listening to you. But pray proceed, and come to the point, for we are not yet entirely agreed.

A: We shall be, I hope, ere long. Since you are such a philosopher, permit me to ask you one question more. Here you have on the one side musicians and poets under the obligation to use the attractions of their art only for the promotion of virtue, and on the other side you have the citizens of your ideal state excluded from exhibitions which give pleasure but not instruction. But what would you do with fortune tellers?

B: They are impostors, who should be expelled from all societies.

A: But yet they do no harm at all. You must bear in mind that we are not referring to sorcerers, so it is not the black art which is to be feared in them.

B: No, I do not fear them at all, because I give no credence to any of their stories: but they do mischief enough by tricking and misleading the public. In my Commonwealth I do not at all tolerate idle people who mislead others, and who have no other occupation than that of talking.

A: But they gain their livelihood by that; and amass money for themselves and their families.

B : No matter; let them find other occupations in order to maintain themselves: it is proper not only to gain a livelihood, but to do it by occupations which are useful to the public. I say the same thing about all those miserable creatures who amuse the passers by with their talk and songs: even if they never lied or did anything disgraceful or bad, they must be got rid of: uselessness alone would render them offenders: the police ought to force them to adopt some respectable mode of life.

A : But those who act tragedies, would you tolerate them? I take for granted, however, that neither illicit love or immodesty is mixed in those tragedies; and furthermore I do not speak as a Christian: reply to me only as a philosopher and a legislator.

B : If those tragedies have not for their object to instruct while giving pleasure, I should condemn them.

A : Good: in that you take precisely the view of Plato, who would not have allowed any tragedies to be represented in his Republic which had not been examined by the judges; so that the people should never see or hear anything which did not serve to strengthen the law and to inspire virtue. In that you are in agreement also with the spirit of the ancient authors, who thought that tragedy should hinge chiefly on two passions; namely, the terror which arises from a view of the deplorable consequences of vice indulged, and the compassion felt for persecuted and patient virtue: that is the idea which Euripides and Sophocles have carried out.

B: You remind me that I have read that last rule in the "Art of Poetry" of M. Boileau.

A: You are right: he is a man who knows thoroughly, not only the theory of poetry, but also the serious object to which philosophy, which is above all the arts, ought to guide the poet.

B: But now, whither are you leading me by all this?

A: I need lead you no further; you are going on of your own accord: indeed you have happily arrived at the desired end. Have you not assured me that you would not tolerate in your Commonwealth any idle people who merely amuse others, and have no other occupation than that of talking? Is it not upon this principle that you would banish those who act tragedies, if instruction is not mingled with pleasure? Shall that be allowed in prose which is not in verse? After that severity, how could you show indulgence to the declaimers who speak only to display their talent and wit?

B: But the declaimers of whom we are speaking have two objects which are praiseworthy.

A: Name them.

B: The first is to maintain themselves: by that means they obtain honourable appointments. Their eloquence gains them reputation, and that draws in its train the fortune which they need.

A : You have already yourself replied to your own objection. Did you not say that it was needful, not only to gain a livelihood, but to gain it by some occupation that is useful to the public? The person who should act a tragedy in which nothing that was instructive was mingled, would be gaining his livelihood: but that fact would not prevent your banishing him. "Take up," you would say to him, "some serious and respectable mode of life; do not merely amuse the citizens. If you wish to derive from them a legitimate profit, labour to some really useful end, or employ yourself to render them more wise and virtuous." Now why would you not say the same thing to the orator?

B : I have another reason to bring forward: the second object of the orator, which I am about to name to you, will explain what it is.

A : Indeed! state it then, if you please.

B : It is that the orator also exerts himself for the advantage of the public.

A : In what respect?

B : He cultures and polishes the intellectual powers by the teaching of eloquence to the people.

A : Listen: if I should invent a useless art, or an imaginary language, from which no advantage could possibly be drawn, should I be of any service to the public by teaching that art or that language?

B: No: because a person is of service to others only in the degree that he teaches them something that is useful.

A: Then you could not possibly prove logically that an orator is of service to the public by teaching eloquence, unless you had already proved that eloquence itself serves some useful purpose. What is the use of the splendid discourses of an orator, if those discourses, fine as they are, bring no practical advantage to the public? " Words," S. Augustine has said, " are made for man, not man for words."*
Those discourses are of use, I know, to him who makes them, because they dazzle his hearers, they cause him who delivers them to be much talked about, and then the public has such bad taste as to reward him for his words, though they are of no use. But ought that eloquence, so mercenary and fruitless to the public, to be permitted in the State that you (by hypothesis) control? A shoemaker at least makes shoes, and could not support his family without the money thus earned by supplying a real need of the public. Thus you see that the commonest occupations have some real object: and can it possibly be that the art of the orator has no real purpose but the amusing of men by words? The only purpose for the gathering of audiences then will be, on the one side to satisfy the curiosity and occupy the idleness of the hearers; and on the

---

* De Doctr. Christ., B. IV., v. 24.

other to feed the vanity and the ambition of him who speaks. For the honour of your Commonwealth never suffer such an abuse as that.

B: Well, then, I acknowledge that the orator ought to have for his object to instruct men and to render them better.

A: Be so good as to keep well in your memory this principle which you have admitted; you will see by and by the consequences which follow from it.

B: But that does not prevent a man, while applying himself to instruct others, from being quite at liberty to acquire at the same time reputation and reward.

A: Let me again remind you that I do not speak here at all as a Christian; I need nothing but philosophy to answer you. Orators are then, I repeat, according to your definition, people whose duty it is to instruct other men and render them better than they are. Here, then, in the first place, all mere declaimers are put out of court. Even panegyrists are not to be tolerated excepting so far as they shall propose models worthy of being imitated and shall render virtue loveable by their praises of it.

B: What! is then a panegyric good for nothing if it is not full of moral teaching?

A: Is not that your own conclusion? The only good reason for speaking is to instruct; a hero is only to be praised that the people may become acquainted with his virtues, and be urged to imitate them, and for the purpose of showing that glory and virtue are inseparable. Therefore all praises that are vague, exaggerated, flattering, ought to be struck out of a panegyric. Not one of those sterile thoughts which are of no service for the instruction of the hearer ought to be suffered there; nothing is admissible but that which tends to make virtue loved. But on the contrary, the greater number of panegyrists seem to praise virtue for no other reason than to praise the men who have practised them, and whose eulogiums they have undertaken to make. Do they desire to praise a man? Then they exalt the virtues which he has practised above all others. But everything has its turn, and on some other occasion they will depreciate the virtues which they had before extolled in favour of some other person whom they wish to flatter. It is upon that principle that I think Pliny to blame. If he had praised Trajan in order to form other heroes similar to him, that would have been an object worthy of an orator. Trajan, great as he was, ought not to have been the entire end of his discourse, but rather an example exhibited to men in order to invite them to be virtuous. When a panegyrist has only the mean object of praising a single man, his work is no more than the flattery of one man appealing to the vanity of another.

B : But what will you say to those poems which

are written in order to praise their heroes? Homer has his Achilles, Virgil his Æneas; would you condemn those two poets?

A : No! but surely you have not examined their poems any farther than the tables of contents. In the Iliad, Achilles is truly the chief hero, but his praise is not the principal object of the poem. He is represented naturally with all his defects, and those very defects are one of the subjects upon which the poet desired to impart instruction to posterity. He sets himself in that work to inspire the Greeks with a love of the glory which is gained in war and combat, and with a fear of disunion as being the obstacle to all great successes. That moral design is visibly marked through the whole poem. It is true that the Odyssey represents in Ulysses a hero more faultless and more accomplished; but this is, so to speak, by chance, and in fact, a man whose predominant character is wisdom, such as was Ulysses, naturally pursues a course of conduct more exalted and uniform than a young man such as Achilles, of a passionate and impetuous nature; thus Homer, both in one case and the other, has only thought of giving a faithful description according to nature. Besides, the Odyssey teems everywhere with a thousand moral instructions for every detail of life, and it is only necessary to read it in order to see that the poet has described a wise and practically able man, who makes his way through all dangers by the help of his wisdom, only in order to teach posterity the good consequences which must attend piety, prudence, and a moral life. Virgil in the Æneid has imitated the Odyssey in the character of his hero. He has made him gentle, pious, and therefore self-possessed in every emergency. It is easy to see that Æneas is not the principal object in his eyes. In that hero he looks forward to the Roman people, whom he makes to be descended from him. He wished to show that people that their origin was divine, that the gods had long ago prepared for them the empire of the world, and in that way to excite the Roman people to sustain by their virtues the glory of their destiny. Among heathens it was not possible to teach any moral lesson of greater importance than that. The only ground on which it might be possible to suspect Virgil of having thought too much of his recompense in his verses, and to have abused his poem for that purpose, is the praise, perhaps somewhat flattering, of Augustus and his family. But I should not be willing to push criticism so far.

B: So then you are not willing that a poet or an orator should honestly try to make his fortune?

A: After our digression upon panegyrics, which will not be useless, we have again returned to our difficulty. The question before us is whether orators ought to be disinterested.

B: I do not think so; you would contradict all the well-known maxims (as to men desiring their own interest).

A : Do you not lay down that in your Commonwealth it should be forbidden to orators to speak anything but the truth, and that they should always speak to instruct and to correct their hearers, and to strengthen the authority of the laws?

B : Yes, no doubt!

A : It follows then that orators must neither hope for anything for their own interest, nor fear anything from their hearers. If you allow of ambitious and mercenary orators, is it likely that they will oppose themselves to all the passions of men? If they are themselves suffering from avarice, from ambition, from effeminacy, how will they be able to minister to the reformation of others? If they are themselves seeking for riches, will they be the fit persons to detach others from them? I am well aware that it would not be right to suffer a virtuous and disinterested man, who serves us in the capacity of an orator, to want for necessary things; but I know, also, that that never happens if he is truly a philosopher, that is to say, of such a character as he needs to be in order to take in hand the mending of the characters of others. He should lead a simple, modest, frugal, and laborious life; he should avoid unnecessary wants, that little which is absolutely needful to him he ought to earn with his own hands; additional supplies ought not to form his recompense, and are not worthy to do so. The public will confer honours upon him and entrust him with authority; but if he is disinterested, and free from the sway of the passions, he will not use that authority except for the public good, and will be prepared to part with it at any time, rather than to preserve it by dissimulation or flattery of the people. Thus the orator, in order to be worthy to exercise persuasion upon the people, ought to be a man who is incorruptible; without that his talent and his very art itself will act as a mortal poison within the Commonwealth, and from this it follows, according to Cicero, that the first and most essential of the qualities which belong to the orator is virtue. He needs probity, which is proof against any temptation, and which serves as a model to all the citizens; without this it is not possible to show belief himself in what he teaches, nor in consequence, to make others believe it.

B : I quite understand the importance of what you urge, but after all, is not a man at liberty to employ his abilities to raise himself to honour?

A : Let us go back always to our first principles. We have agreed that eloquence and the profession of the orator should be devoted to the instruction and the improvement of the people. In order to perform this freely and successfully a man must be disinterested; he must instil into others disdain for riches, for enjoyments, and of death; he must inspire modesty, frugality, disinterestedness, zeal for the public good, and inviolable attachment to the laws; and all this must show itself no less in his life and character than in his discourses. How can a man who endeavours to please for the sake of his own advancement, and who therefore wants to make use of everybody, exercise such an authority as this over minds? And even if he should say all that is proper to be said, is it to be supposed that belief will be inspired by the speech of a man who does not appear to believe it himself?

B: But he does nothing wrong in seeking to gain a fortune of which I take it for granted that he has need.

A: That matters not; let him seek in other paths of life the means of livelihood. There are other professions which will save him from the dangers of poverty; if he needs anything, and is reduced to beg it from the public, he is not the fit person to be an orator. In your Commonwealth would you choose poor and starving persons for judges? Would you not fear that their necessities would reduce them to some dishonourable compliance? Would you not rather choose persons of consideration, and who would not therefore be tempted by their necessities?

B: I certainly would.

A: For a similar reason would you not choose for orators, that is to say for masters whose duty it is to instruct, correct, and train the minds of the people, persons who had no need of anything, and were therefore disinterested? And if there were others who had ability for all kinds of occupations, but who had also private interests which they wished to serve, would you not defer to employ their eloquence until they had attained the objects they so desired, and thus need be no longer suspected of some interested motive when speaking publicly?

B: But it seems to me that the experience of our age proves that an orator may inculcate morality with great power, without abandoning all interest as to his future. Could there possibly be moral sketches more severe than those now before the public? Yet they do not arouse anger, they even give pleasure; and the person to whom they are due is continually rising in the world by their means.

A: Moral sketches have no persuasive power whatever when they are supported neither by principles nor by good examples. Whom did you ever know to be converted by such? People soon grow accustomed to hear these descriptions; they are only a succession of striking images made to pass before the eyes; such discourses are listened to as if a satire were being read; people look at the speaker as one who acts well a kind of comedy, and take much more notice of what he does than what he says. If he is ambitious, vain, moved by interested motives, fond of a luxurious life; if he himself does not relinquish any of the things which he bids others relinquish; people may listen to him as a matter of ceremony; but they will believe and act in the same way as he. And which is even worse, they will come to think that persons of that profession do not speak in good faith; they will disparage their ministry, and will not be persuaded of the sincerity of others, who speak with genuine and honest zeal.

B: I allow that your principles are thoroughly consistent with each other, and that they gain upon the mind when examined with attention; but is it by the pure zeal of Christian piety that you say all these things?

A: It is not necessary to be a Christian to think thus, though one must be a Christian to practise them well; since only Divine grace can repress the love of self: but it is only needful to be a person of reasonable mind to recognize that these things are true. As often as I have cited Socrates or Plato, you have been willing to defer to their authority: but now that you are beginning to be convinced by reason, and that you have no more need of authority, what will you say if I show you that this reasoning is employed by them also?

B: By them! is it possible! I shall be well pleased indeed.

A: Plato introduces Socrates as conversing with an orator named Gorgias, and with a pupil of

Gorgias named Callicles. This Gorgias was a man of high reputation; Isocrates, of whom we have said so much, was his pupil. This Gorgias was the first, says Cicero, who boasted that he was able to speak eloquently about every subject: afterwards the Greek rhetoricians imitated that vanity. Let us return to the dialogue of Gorgias and Callicles. These two men discoursed elegantly upon all things, according to the method of the former; they were persons of that fine genius which sparkles in conversation, and they had no other object than to speak well; but it appears that they were wanting in that which Socrates sought for in men; that is to say, true principles of morality, and exact and serious rules in reasoning. After the author has skilfully held up to ridicule that character of genius, he introduces Socrates, who, while he seems to jest with them, pleasantly reduces the two orators to the condition of not being able to say in what eloquence consists. Then Socrates shows that rhetoric, that is to say, the art of those orators, was not truly an art at all. He defines art as "a regulated discipline, which teaches men to do something useful to make them better than they are." Thus he shows that it is only *liberal* arts which are entitled to the name; and that these degenerate whenever they are employed to any other end than to form men to virtue. He shows that rhetoricians have not that object at all; that even Themistocles and Pericles did not keep it in view, and consequently were not true orators. He says that those celebrated men thought only of persuading the Athenians to make harbours, to build fortifications, or to gain victories. They have, he says, only rendered their fellow citizens rich, powerful, and warlike, and were afterwards ill-treated by them; which return was only what they might have expected. If, by their eloquence, they had rendered their fellow citizens good, their reward, he says, would have been certain. A person who makes men good and virtuous is sure not to find them ungrateful after his labour; for virtue and ingratitude are incompatible. It is not needful to recall all that he says about the uselessness of that rhetoric, because all that I have said to you upon it, as from myself, is drawn from him; it will be of more service to relate what he says respecting the evils which empty declaimers occasion in a State.

B: I quite understand that those rhetoricians were to be feared in the Greek Republics, where they might win over the people and usurp the government.

A: In fact, it is principally of that inconvenience that Socrates speaks; but the principles which he enunciates on that occasion may be much further extended. Nevertheless, when we speak here, you and I, of organizing a Commonwealth, it applies not only to States where the people govern, but to every State, whether democratic, that which is governed by a number of chiefs (aristocratic), or monarchical; so that I do not refer at all to the form of government; in all countries the rules of Socrates are equally applicable.

B: Explain them, then, if you please.

A: He says that man being composed of body and mind, it is needful to cultivate both the one and the other. There are two arts for the cultivation of the mind, and two for that of the body. The two for the mind are the science of laws and jurisprudence. By the science of laws he understands all those principles of philosophy which direct how to regulate the characters and sentiments of individuals, or of the whole State. Jurisprudence is the remedy made use of to repress injustice and bad faith in citizens; it is by it that lawsuits are decided and crimes punished. Thus the science of laws is of use to prevent evil; and jurisprudence to correct it.* There are two similar arts for the

---

* " There is scarcely a law in God's code but has its parallel in man's code; hardly a demand made by God for the government of His commonwealth, but man also makes for the government of his commonwealth. The preacher, who is versed in the fundamentals of Blackstone, Kent, Chitty, Parsons, *et al.*, can show : 1. That law is necessary ; 2 That society has a right to protect itself; 3. That self-preservation is a law written even upon the code of conscience ; 4. That in a world where sin is so slightly offensive, and rulers have pledged so little, it is often found necessary to pass sentence of perpetual banishment, imprisonment for life, and death even; 5. That belief or skepticism on the part of the culprit concerning the law, does not, in the least, lessen

body: gymnastics, which exercises it, renders it healthy, well-proportioned, active, vigorous, full of strength and grace (you know, do you not, that the Ancients made astonishing use of that art, which we have lost); and medicine, which cures the body when it has lost health. Gymnastics are for the body what moral philosophy is for the soul; it forms and perfects it. Medicine, again, is to the body what jurisprudence is to the mind; it corrects it, and restores it to health. But that institution, which was so unsullied, has been altered, says Socrates. In the place of a solid practical philosophy has been substituted the vain subtilty of the sophists: false philosophers who abuse the forms of reasoning, and who, being without the principles which tend truly to the public good, direct their efforts to the promotion of their private interests. To jurisprudence, he says again, has succeeded the conceit of the rhetoricians, people whose only wish is to please, and excite admiration; instead of jurisprudence, which should be the medicine of the soul, and which should only be used to heal the

---

his culpability nor the certainty of his paying the full penalty; 6. That his inability to comprehend all the whys and wherefores of the law by which he is adjudged a criminal does not detract one whit from the baseness of his deflection, nor the deplorableness of his situation; 7. That all his fine theorizing about what the law *should be* or *should not be*, does not affect the law that *is* and which the judge is bound to follow in passing sentence upon him. Here, too, the great central doctrine of the Atonement finds its fullest, and most unanswerable unfoldment."—J. M. DRIVER.

passions of men, are seen the exhibitions of false orators, who think only of their own reputation. To gymnastics, adds he again, has been made to succeed the art of sophisticating and disguising the body, as to give to it a false and deceptive attractiveness; instead of which, all that should be sought is a simple and natural beauty, which comes of the health and proportion of all the limbs; and that is acquired and retained only by exercise and the observance of rule. In the place of medicine has come all manner of delicious viands, and *ragoûts*, which stimulate the appetite; and when a man is full of unhealthy humours, instead of purging him to restore health, and by health the appetite, they put force upon nature, and create an artificial appetite by various expedients contrary to temperance. It is in these terms that Socrates remarks upon the disorder of the manners of his time; and he concludes by saying that orators, who, with the view of curing men, ought to tell them even disagreeable truths, and that with authority, and to administer to them, so to speak, bitter medicines, have, on the contrary, acted towards the soul as cooks do towards the body. Their rhetoric has been nothing but the art of making delicacies (so to speak) to flutter the appetites of sick men; they have given themselves no trouble except to please, to arouse curiosity and admiration; they have spoken only for that purpose. He finishes by demanding: Where are the citizens whom these rhetoricians have cured of their evil habits? Where the people whom they have rendered temperate and virtuous? Would you not think that you were listening to a man of our own time, who was speaking of present abuses? After having heard the sentiments of that wise heathen, what do you say of that eloquence which sets itself only to please and to make fine pictures, when it should, as he has himself said, burn and cut to the quick, so as seriously to seek a cure by bitter remedies and a severe rule? But judge of these things for yourself; what would you find praiseworthy in a physician who, when you were in the extremity of illness, and it was his duty to prescribe suitable remedies for you, amused himself with turning elegant phrases and developing some fine theory? What would you think of a barrister who, when pleading a cause on the event of which was suspended all the property of your family, or even your own life, should put on the airs of a man of wit, and supplement his pleadings with flowers and ornaments of wit and humour, instead of reasoning with force, and exciting the sympathy of the judges? The love of goods and of life makes that seem ridiculous enough to us; but the indifference which is apparent with regard to goodness and to religion causes this not to be at all remarked in orators, who ought to be the censors and the physicians of the people. What we have seen of the opinion of Socrates ought to make us ashamed.

B: I see now very well that, according to your principles, orators ought to be the defenders of the laws and the teachers of virtue to the people; but legal eloquence among the Romans did not reach that point.

A: That was without doubt the proposed object to it; orators were to protect innocence and the rights of private persons, when they had no occasion to bring forward the general needs of the Commonwealth; it followed from this that the profession was so honoured, and that Cicero gives so high an idea of the true orator.

B: But let us see, then, in what manner those orators ought to speak: I beg you to express to me your views upon that point.

A: I shall not say anything to you about my own views: I shall continue to expound to you the rules that the ancients give us. I shall mention only the principal things, for you would not have leisure for me to explain to you consecutively, in detail, the numerous precepts almost infinitely of rhetoric. Many of them are useless; you have, no doubt, looked into the books in which they are amply set forth: let us be satisfied with mentioning the most important. Plato, in that dialogue in which he introduces Socrates conversing with Phædrus, shows that the great fault of rhetoricians is that they seek for the art of persuading before they have learned by the principles of philosophy what are the truths that should be taught to others. He would have the orator commence by the study of mankind in general, and afterwards to apply himself to gaining knowledge of the individual persons to whom he may have to speak. Thus he ought to know what man is, what is his chief end, what are his true interests, what are the elements of his nature, that is to say, body and spirit; the true way of making him happy: what are his passions, what excesses they are liable to run into, how they can be regulated, and how usefully aroused so as to make man love that which is good; what are the rules calculated to make him live at peace and which tend to hold society together. After that general study comes the particular: he ought to be acquainted with the laws and customs of his country, and how these are expressive of the national character: the manners of each rank, the differences of education, the interests and the prejudices which rule in the age in which he lives, the means of instructing and of raising up minds. You see that these various kinds of knowledge comprehend all the most real and well established elements of politics and philosophy. In this way Plato shows that only a philosopher can be a true orator: it is in that sense that we must explain all that he has said in the dialogue of Gorgias, against rhetoricians; that is to say, against the class of men who have made the speaking skilfully, so as to persuade others into an art without giving themselves the trouble to learn in principle that which it is their duty to try to persuade men of. Thus, in fact, the whole of the art, according to Plato, consists in knowing well that which we ought to inculcate, in being well acquainted with the passions of men, and the mode of arousing them for any particular object. Cicero says almost the same thing. He seems to urge, in the first place, that the orator should be ignorant of nothing, because he may have to speak upon anything, and that he can never speak well (as he says after Socrates) of that which he does not know well. But this he afterwards reduces, in consideration of pressing necessity and of the shortness of life, to the most essential kinds of knowledge. He is of opinion that an orator should at least know well all that part of philosophy which concerns manners, permitting him to neglect only the curiosities of astrology and mathematics: especially he thinks that the orator should be acquainted with the composition of man and the nature of his passions, because the purpose of oratory is to arouse them for various objects.*

---

* "All this part of the argument pre-supposes a state of things in which society in general was much more dependent upon the Pulpit (or the Bar) for instruction than at the present time. The Press, with its powerful function as a teacher in every department of knowledge, did not then exist. Nevertheless, the argument for perfectness of culture in the Clergy is indefinitely strengthened, now that, as an American writer (PROF. M. D. BISBEE) remarks: 'After he has done his best, the preacher knows that every hearer can sit at home and read a better sermon. Commentaries, newspapers, libraries, and the multitudinous

He requires the knowledge of the laws from the orator as the foundation of all his discourses; only he allows that he need not have passed his life in a profound study of the details of causes, since he can, when needful, have recourse to those deeply learned in the law to supply any lack of knowledge in himself. He requires, as does Plato, that the orator should be a good logician: that he should know how to define, prove, or disprove the most subtle sophisms. He says that it destroys rhetoric to separate it from philosophy, and makes of orators puerile declaimers, wanting in judgment.* He asks

---

circles of information, leave the minister no exclusive fields of knowledge. His only resource is to make more vivid what is already known, and to transmute knowledge into life. Then the present, to a singular extent, is a reading age. Most people prefer to sit and read rather than listen, and there is much in this that is profitable. Multitudes are acquiring knowledge and forming convictions in this way, but it is making the work of the pulpit more difficult.'

'There was a time, not so far ago, when the Sunday sermon was almost the only intellectual food which the majority of the population had the means of enjoying. Just think of the difference at the present moment! Think how the intellectual appetite is actually gorged and drenched by the provisions meted out to it! Think of the newspapers, the magazines, the cheap novels, the miscellaneous literature of all sorts and descriptions! The Sunday sermon, instead of being the main item, is now but a comparatively small one of what is poured, week by week, into the minds and imaginations of our people."
—TWELLS, *Colloquies on Preaching*, p. 236.

* "For me, readers, although I cannot say that I am utterly untrain'd in those rules which best rhetoricians have given, or unacquainted with those examples which the prime authors of eloquence have written in any learned tongue; yet true eloquence I find to be none but the serious

not only for an exact knowledge of all the principles of ethics, but for a special study of antiquity. He recommends the reading of the ancient Greek writers; that historians should be studied, not only for their style, but to acquire the facts of history; and especially he requires the study of the poets, because of the close relation that there is between the figures of poetry and those of eloquence. In one word, he inculcates everywhere that the orator ought to store his mind with knowledge before attempting to speak in public. I believe that I recall his very words, so often have I read them, and so deep an impression have they made upon me: you would be surprised at the extent of the demands they make. "The orator," he says, "ought to have the subtlety of the dialectician, the knowledge of a philosopher, the diction, almost, of a poet, the voice and the gestures of the greatest actors." Consider now what an amount of preparation would be needed for such a result as that.

C: In point of fact, I have remarked on many occasions, that what is most wanting in many orators, who have nevertheless much ability, is a

---

and hearty love of truth; and that whose mind soever is fully possest with a fervent desire to know good things, and with the dearest charity to infuse the knowledge of them into others, when such a man would speak, his words (by what I can express) like so many nimble and airy servitors, trip about him at command, and in well-order'd files, as he would wish, fall aptly into their own places."

—MILTON's *Apology for Smectymnuus.*

store of knowledge: their minds appear to be empty: it was evident enough that they had difficulty in finding sufficient material to complete their discourse: it even seems that they do not speak because they are in possession of truths, but that they are seeking for truths only because they wish to speak.

A : That is what Cicero says of those people: they live always, as it were, from day to day without any provision beforehand, and notwithstanding all their efforts, their discourses appear always starved and thin. A man has not time to give himself three months of preparation before delivering a discourse; those special preparations, however painstaking they may be, are of necessity very imperfect, and a skilled person easily finds out those who are weak in this respect. Many years of study are needed to provide for oneself an abundant store of knowledge. After that general preparation has once been made, special preparation costs little trouble: but the speaker who, instead of going through this careful preliminary training, applies himself only to unconnected subjects, is obliged to dwell upon phrases and antitheses, to treat only of the commonplace, to deal only in vague statements, to weave together threads of thought which have nothing to do with each other. He is unable, for want of study, to display the true principles and connections of things, he is limited to reasons which are superficial and often false; he is not capable of showing the real proportions of truths, because all general truths form, necessarily, an organized whole, and it is needful to be acquainted with almost all of them in order to treat solidly of any one.

C: Nevertheless, most of those who speak in public acquire great reputation without any greater stock of knowledge than that you regard as so insufficient.

A: It is true that they may be applauded by women, and by the unthinking portion of the world, who easily allow themselves to be dazzled: but such popularity is never more than a certain caprice of fashion, and needs ever to be upheld by some clique. People who know the object and the rules of eloquence feel only disgust and disdain for discourses which are all "in the air," and are wearied excessively by them.

B: You would make a man wait very long before speaking in public: his youth would be passed before he had acquired the store of knowledge which you think needful, and he would no longer be of an age to exercise this function of speaking.

A: I would have him exercise it sufficiently soon, for I do not lose sight of the power which comes of experience; but I should not wish that, under the pretext of exercising it, he should throw himself at first into multifarious employments which would take away from a young man the liberty of study. He should undoubtedly have, from time to time, opportunities to try his powers, but the study of good books should for a long time be his principal occupation.

C: I think you are right, and that recalls to my memory a preacher, a friend of mine, who used to live, as you said, from day to day; he did not give any consideration to a subject until it was his duty to treat upon it: then he would shut himself up in his study, he would turn over the leaves of the Concordance, Combéfis, Polyanthea,* some volumes of sermons which he had bought, and certain collections which he had made of detached passages which he had met with by chance.

A: You easily understand that all that sort of thing could not possibly make a skilful preacher. In such a condition as that a man can be sure of nothing, he can never speak with power, he has an appearance of borrowing everything and of always making quotations, never of being himself the source of any sentiment which he expresses. A person does injustice to himself who has so much impatience to make himself known.

B: Before you leave us, will you tell us what, in your opinion, is the great effect of eloquence.

A: Plato says that a discourse is eloquent in proportion to the effect it produces on the mind of the hearer: according to that rule you can estimate exactly every discourse that you hear. An address

---

* These were the popular " Sermon Helps " of the day.

or sermon which leaves you unmoved, which does not touch the depth of your feelings, which tends only to afford you intellectual gratification, is not truly eloquent at all.* Will you hear the opinion of Cicero, which is the same as that of Plato, upon this point? He will tell you that all the force of oratory ought to be directed to no other object than to stir and influence the hidden springs of feeling which nature has set in the heart and mind of man. Therefore look into your own self in order to learn whether the orator to whom you listen speaks well. If they make a strong impression upon you; if they make your soul heedful and sensitive to what they say; if they warm your feelings and carry you out of and above yourself, you may safely believe that they have attained the point of eloquence. But if,

---

* "A friend of mine, a layman, was once in the company of a very eminent preacher, then in the decline of life. My friend happened to remark what a comfort it must be to him to think of all the good he had done by his gift of eloquence. The eyes of the old man filled with tears, and he said: 'You little know! You little know! If I ever turned one heart from the ways of disobedience to the wisdom of the just, God has withheld the assurance from me. I have been admired, and flattered, and run after; but how gladly I would forget all that, to be told of a single soul I have been instrumental in saving.' The eminent preacher entered into his rest. There was a great funeral. Many pressed around the grave who had oftentimes hung entranced upon his lips. My friend was there, and by his side was a stranger who was so deeply moved that, when all was over, my friend said to him: 'You knew him, I suppose?' 'Knew him!' was the reply, 'No, I never spoke to him, but I owe to him my soul.'"

—TWELLS, *Colloquies*, p. 12.

instead of softening your heart, or inspiring you with strong feeling, they merely please you and make you admire the justness of their thoughts and the brilliancy of their phrases, you may conclude that they are but pretenders to oratory.

B: Pray stay a little longer, and permit me to ask you some further questions.

A: I should be glad to do so, for I have had much pleasure in our conversation, but I have business to attend to which will not admit of delay. I will, however, see you again to-morrow, and we will then, if you please, go on with the consideration of this matter at greater leisure.

B: Adieu then, sir, until to-morrow.

Second Dialogue.

The orator, in order to attain his object, must PROVE, *must* POURTRAY, *and must* IMPRESS *the hearer. Principles of the art of oratory. Observations on the method of learning sermons and delivering them by heart, also on divisions and sub-divisions. The orator ought severely to exclude frivolous ornaments from his discourse.*

B: It is very good of you to have returned so punctually; our conversation of yesterday has left us impatient to continue the subject.

C: As for me, I have come in haste, fearing to be late, for I did not wish to lose any part of the conversation.

A: Interviews like this of ours are by no means without their use for those who are calm and candid; we communicate our thoughts to each other, and each brings forward the best results of his reading. And on my part, gentlemen, I profit greatly by discussing the subject with you, and you are good enough to pardon my freedom of speech.

B: You are very courteous; but for my part it is only fair to confess that I should have been, I am convinced, still sunk in many errors without your assistance. I beg of you to be so good as to complete my deliverance from them.

A : Your mistakes, if you permit me to speak of them as such, are those of the greater number of respectable people who have not investigated these matters.

B : I beg of you then to set me completely right: we shall have a thousand things to say, so let us lose no time, but come at once to the point without further preface.

A : Of what were we speaking yesterday when we separated? If I remember rightly it was of the object to be contemplated by the orator.

C : You were speaking of eloquence, which consists entirely in touching and influencing the hearer.

B : Yes, I scarcely understood that; what did you mean?

A : I will explain. What would you say of a man who should persuade without proving? Such a person would not be a true orator; but still he would be able to allure and lead away other men, having the trick of making them agree with him without showing them that what he would persuade them of was the truth. Such a man would be dangerous in the State; we have already seen that in the argument of Socrates.

B : I allow that.

A : But what would you say of a man who should demonstrate that which was true, but in a manner dry and bare, although exact; who should put his arguments in correct form, or who should make use of the method of mathematicians in his public discourses, without adding anything vivid, striking, or figurative? Would he be an orator?

B: No, he would be only a philosopher.

A: To make an orator then, it is necessary to take a philosopher, that is to say a man who knows how to demonstrate the truth, and to add to the exactness of his reasonings, the beauty and the vehemence of a varied discourse; and thus you will have made an orator.

B: Yes, no doubt.

A: That shows precisely the difference between Philosophy, which demonstrates, and Eloquence, which persuades.

B: I do not quite understand you.

A: I mean that the philosopher's only aim is to convince; but the orator, besides convincing, persuades.

B: Still, I do not altogether follow you. When the hearer is convinced, what is there left to be done?

A: You will see what remains to be done if you suppose an orator and a metaphysician, each proving to you the existence of God. The one will give you simply a demonstration, which does not pass at all out of the sphere of speculation; the other will add to that everything calculated to excite in you the feelings of devotion and love towards that holy and glorious Being whose existence is thus shown: that is called *persuasion*.

B : Now I understand your view.

A : Cicero was quite right in saying that philosophy ought never to be separated from eloquence; for the ability to persuade is, without knowledge and wisdom, simply pernicious; while without this art of persuasion wisdom is unable to win over the hearts of men, so that they shall apply themselves unto virtue. It is well just to remark that in passing, in order that we may understand how greatly mistaken were the people of the last century. There were, on one side, men of letters who cared only for the purity of style, and the polish of the periods, in books; these people, being without solid principles of doctrine, with all their culture and learning, were for the most part freethinkers. On the other side there were scholastic theologians, dry and thorny, who put forward truths in a manner so disagreeable and so little calculated to attract attention, that they repelled almost everybody.*

---

* "If we go back to the period of the Renaissance, we find the Church, instead of putting herself at the head of the great movements of science, discovery and manufacture, spending her time, as Father Barry says, in fruitless discussions, chanting lovely anthems and weaving copes of broidered gold in cathedral stalls, while commerce and inventive industry were calling into existence huge black cities and millions of machine-made proletariat, who stand outside, brawling and

Pardon me this digression. I will now return to our subject. Persuasion has this, in addition to simple conviction, that not only does it display the truth, but displays it in attractive colours, and disposes men to be in favour of it. Thus in eloquence everything consists in adding to the solid proof of a proposition the means of interesting the hearer in it, and enlisting his feelings in favour of that which is proposed to him. He is inspired with indignation against ingratitude, horror against cruelty, compassion for misery, love for virtue, and so on. That is what Plato calls working on the soul of the hearer, and influencing his feelings. Do you still follow me?

B: Yes, I quite understand, and I see clearly that eloquence is not at all a frivolous expedient for dazzling men by brilliant discourses: it is a very serious art, and of great usefulness for the promotion of goodness.

A: And on that account Cicero says that though he had known many good speakers, that is to say, men who spoke in an agreeable and effective manner; he had scarcely ever known a true orator, that is, a man who knows how to enter into the hearts of others, and to lead and influence them as he wills.

---

drinking, tearing their bread from one another, working with despair in their hearts the while, as many hours of the day and night as they can toil and live, refusing to see any salvation in Christ, as represented in the Church of the period."—Prof. M. D. Bisbee.

B: I am not surprised at that, and I am quite sure that scarcely any one ever aims at that result. I confess to you that even Cicero, who lays down that rule, seems to me to wander from it sometimes. What do you say of all those flowers of rhetoric with which he has adorned his Orations? That appears to me to be merely the play of intellectual ingenuity, which takes no hold upon the feelings at all.

A: There is a distinction to be borne in mind. Those orations which Cicero wrote while he was yet young, and in which he is principally concerned to establish a reputation for himself, often have that defect. It is very evident in them that he was much more engrossed with the wish to be admired than with the thought of the justice of his cause. That will always be the case, when a litigant shall employ, to plead his cause, a man who cares for the matter only as a means of making a brilliant entrance into his profession, and we know well that pleading among the Romans was often turned into nothing but gaudy declamation. But after all, it must be allowed that even in the most flowery of those harangues, there is much that is touching and persuasive. It is not, however, at that class of Cicero's writings that we ought to look in order to become well acquainted with him, but at the orations which he composed at a later period of his life on behalf of the Republic in its time of need, when experience of great affairs, the love of liberty, and fear of the calamities with which it was threatened, urged him to efforts worthy of an orator. When he strove to sustain expiring liberty, to arouse the whole Republic against his enemy Antony, you no longer find him striving after antitheses and witticisms; then he is truly eloquent. All he says is direct and unstudied, as he says himself in his treatise *De Oratore* that a speaker ought to be when he desires to be forcible and vehement: he is a man who simply seeks in unsophisticated and natural appeals and persuasions, all that is capable of arresting, of animating, and of influencing the nature of man.

C: You have often spoken of epigrams; I should be glad to know precisely what you intend by this term; for I confess that I am not always able to distinguish epigrams from other enrichments of a discourse: and it seems to me that this play of wit occurs in all great efforts of oratory.

A: Excuse me: there are, even according to Cicero, expressions in which the whole of the enrichment comes from their own emphasis and from the nature of the subject.

C: I do not understand at all these technical terms; explain to me, if you please, in a simple way, how I can distinguish a substantial and valid ornament of oratory from a mere epigram.

A: Only reading and observation will teach you

to distinguish : there are a hundred different kinds of epigrams and witticisms.

C : But still, pardon me for persisting: what is the broad and general mark (of the epigram): is it affectation ?

A : It is not every kind of affectation : but that particular kind which is prompted by the wish to please, and to display one's own cleverness.

C : That is something gained : but I should be glad of marks more precise still, to aid me to discriminate between them.

A : Well! here is one with which perhaps you will be satisfied. I have already said that eloquence consists, not only in proving truths, but still more in the art of arousing the feelings and sentiments. In order to arouse them, recourse must be had to descriptions of characters or scenes that are of a touching character : thus I conclude that the whole of eloquence is reducible to these three elements : to *prove,* to *portray*, to *impress*. Thoughts, however brilliant, which do not conduce to one of these three ends are, all of them, only epigrams or conceits.*

C : What do you mean by " to portray " ? I do not at all understand that term as applied to rhetoric.

---

* "As for jest, there be certain things which ought to be privileged from it; namely religion, matters of state, great persons, any man's present business of importance, and any case that deserveth pity. Yet there be some that think their wits have been asleep, except they dart

A : To portray, is not merely to describe scenes or events, but to represent them with all their circumstances, in a manner so vivid and distinct, that the auditor almost imagines that he beholds them. For example, a frigid historian, who was describing the death of Dido, would content himself with saying : " She was so overwhelmed with grief after the departure of Æneas, that she was not able to endure her life : she went up to the roof of her palace, placed herself on a funeral pile, and killed herself." In listening to these words you learn the fact, but you do not *see* it. But now listen to Virgil ; he puts the whole scene before your eyes. Is it not true that when he accumulates all the circumstances of that despair; when he *shows* you Dido in her frenzy, with her countenance, on which death is already painted ; when he repeats her soliloquy at the sight of the portrait and of the

---

out something that is piquant and to the quick. That is a vein which should be bridled : ' Parce, puer, stimulis, et fortius utere horis.' "

—Bacon's *Essays, xxxii.*

"Humour is no new thing in the pulpit. There is humour in the Bible; there are flashes of it among the Fathers. It gleamed from Wyclif's solemn eyes. Luther broke into it, often wildly enough. In Latimer it was a full and ceaseless fountain. Zwingli did not disdain it. Erasmus wielded it with power. The grim earnestness of Bunyan was suffused with its brightness. Abraham-à-Sancta Clara made it the fashion in the seventeenth century of all the Roman Catholic pulpits of Germany. In religious controversy how Abelard and Pascal triumphed with it ; how Sidney Smith and John Henry Newman irradiated with it the weak places of the positions, by them so vehemently attacked."

—C. J. Little, D.D.

sword; your imagination transports you to Carthage? You fancy you see the fleet of the Trojans sailing away from the shore, and the inconsolable queen: you enter, in fact, into all the sentiments of which you seem to be in truth spectators. You are no longer listening to Virgil: you are too intent upon the last words of the unhappy Dido to think of him. The poet has disappeared; but you no longer see anything but what he makes you see, nor hear anything but what he causes you to hear. See the power of portrayal, of illusion!* That is the cause why a painter and a poet have so much in common: one paints for the eyes, the other for the ears: and both one and the other ought to carry objects direct to the imagination. I have quoted an example from a poet to give you a clearer comprehension of what I mean: since the power of portrayal is still more strong and vivid in poets than in orators. Poetry does not differ from simple eloquence, except that it depicts with enthusiasm, and with more grand and bold strokes. Prose has its pictures, though they are less glowing; and without these pictures it is not possible to warm the

---

* "The more you lose your isolated self, and the thoughts and feelings which cluster round it, and take instead into you the thoughts and feelings of others, the richer and the more varied, the more complex and the more interesting, and therefore the more vividly individual, becomes your being. . . . It is in such a moment when, as it were, you find your individuality outside of you in the being of the universe, that you are most individual, and most able to feel your being, though not to think it."—STOPFORD A. BROOKE, *Sermon on Individuality*.

imagination of the hearer, nor to excite his feelings. A simple narrative does not touch and arouse : it is needful not only to inform the hearers of facts, but to render these living before them, and to strike their senses by a perfect representation of all that was touching in the way they took place."*

C: I had never understood all that before. I see now perfectly that what you call *portrayal* is essential to eloquence ; but you would also have me believe that there is no eloquence at all without poetry.

A : You may firmly believe it, if only you take away from poetry the versification ; that is, the measured line of a limited number of syllables, in which the poet is obliged to cramp his thoughts. The ignorant vulgar believe this to be the essential part of poetry ; they suppose a man to be a poet who has written in measured lines. But on the contrary, many people write verses without the least poetry in them ; and many others are full of poetry without writing verses. Put versification

---

* An obvious limitation of this principle, with regard to descriptions of scenery, is stated below : "It is hazardous to introduce extended descriptions of natural scenery into sermons, lest the personal experience with which they are connected be rather hidden than illustrated by them ; and lest—as has sometimes happened—the sermon itself shall seem to have been constructed with reference to them, as if a house had been planned to match a mantel-piece. But occasionally they add to a discourse a vivid and memorable moral force, as well as rare pictorial beauty."—Dr. R. S. STORRS.

then out of the question. For all the rest, poetry is nothing else than the production of a powerful impression or illusion in which nature is portrayed. No one, who has not this genius for portrayal, will ever impress facts and truths on the minds of his hearers : all will be dry, uninteresting, and tiresome. Since the first sin, man has been, so to speak, buried in what he sees and hears : it is a great evil that it is so : and he cannot be long attentive to that which is wholly of an abstract character.*

---

* "Plain speech should be coupled with plain thought. The thoughts which serve as starting points, should always be simple, natural and popular. The people do not understand abstractions or the speculations of reason, which are to them a strange language. You should start from the known to lead them to the unknown. That is the mathematical and logical method. You must begin with sensible, visible, and above all with actual things, in order to draw them gently towards spiritual and invisible things, and to the life that is to come. By adopting this course, you may conduct them far onward and elevate them to great heights, even to the sublimest aspirations of heart and soul. . . . As we have already said, by way of example : first exhibit religion to them as grand, good, and lovely, then as true and divine; winding up by fervently and energetically insisting on the necessity of submission to its moral law."

—L'Abbe Mullois, *Cours d'Eloquence Sacreé Populaire*, p. 149.

"A crowd always tires of the abstract ; but the concrete fatigues it also, if only serious or sublime. Hence the rifts of humour in natures charged with solemn message and responsibility are sunshine and relief, enhancing and not diminishing the preacher's power. A wrath that would be blinding in its full intensity, dissolved to lambent mockery, sharpens and strengthens the sight by the rest it gives to overwrought emotion. So it was with Theodore Parker : so it was with Sancta Clara in his nobler days. Or the argument that crushed attention rather than opposition, suddenly relieves us of its weight and dances

All the instruction which we wish to convey to the spirit must be given to the body: and the body requires concrete and inviting ideas to engage its attention. From this it followed that soon after the fall of the human race, poetry and idolatry, always joined together, made up the entire religion of the early races of mankind. But let us not diverge farther. You see clearly that poetry, that is to say, the vivid realization and depicting of facts and truths is, as it were, the very soul of eloquence.

C: But if true orators are poets, it seems to me that poets are also orators: for poetry has a persuasive power.

A: No doubt they have the same object: the difference between them lies in what I have already noticed. Poets have enthusiasm in a higher degree than orators, and this renders their expressions even more lofty, vivid, and daring. Do you remember what I have so often observed to you about Cicero?

C: Do you mean that—?

A: That the orator ought to have *almost* the diction of the poets;* that *almost* says everything.

---

before us a tricksy epigram, its meaning flashing from its face and making all that went before blaze with its significance. Such, since the days of Wyclif, has been the humour of many of the noblest preachers in the English tongue. But humour is full of peril *to the preacher.*"

—C. J. LITTLE, D.D.

* " Omnes enim, sive artis sunt loci, sive ingenii cujusdam atque prudentiæ, qui modo insunt in ea re, de qua scribimus, anquirentibus

C: I begin to understand: all that is growing clear to my mind. But let us go back to what you have promised us.

A: You will soon quite understand. Of what service in a discourse can anything be which does not keep towards one of these three things: to prove, to describe, or to affect and persuade?

C: It will serve to please the hearer.

A: Let us distinguish. That which serves to please in order to persuade is good. Proofs which are solid and well expressed doubtless please; the natural and vivacious appeals of the orator have much that is attractive; faithful and animated descriptions have their charms. Thus the three elements which we allow in eloquence please, but they do not limit themselves to pleasing. The question to be decided is whether we shall approve thoughts and expressions which tend *only* to please, and have no effect more solid. It is they which I call *jeux d'esprit*. Remember then, always, that I approve of all the graces of discourse which are serviceable for persuasion: I reject only those in which the orator, from his own self-love, has been

---

nobis, omnique acie ingenii contemplautibus ostendunt se et occurrunt; omnesque sententiæ, verbaque omnia, quæ sunt cujusque generis maxime illustria, sub acumen styli subeant et succedant necesse est; tum ipsa collocatio conformatioque verborum perficitur in scribendo, non poetico, sed quodam oratorio numero et modo."—CICERO: *De Oratore, lib. i. cap. xxxiii.*

desirous to exhibit himself, and amuse the hearer by his own talent, instead of occupying his mind with the subject of the discourse. Thus it appears to me that not only ought witticisms (which are mere plays upon words) to be condemned, since they are cold and puerile, but also all mere plays of thought; that is to say, those whose only effect is to sparkle and astonish, since they have in them nothing tangible and calculated to persuade.

C: I should willingly agree to that. But would you not, by this severity, lop off the principal ornaments of discourse?

A : Do you not find that Virgil and Homer are sufficiently agreeable as authors? Do you think they could be more attractive? Yet you will not find in their writings any *jeux d'esprit:* only simple language, everywhere natural, and art everywhere carefully concealed: you will not find in them a single word which appears to have been used to display the genius of the poet; he makes it a point of honour not to appear at all himself, in order to occupy you with the things which he describes; just as a painter aims to put before your eyes forests, mountains, torrents, distances, buildings: the actions and adventures of men and their various passions, without your being able to remark the separate strokes of the brush: art would be coarse and contemptible in proportion as it were suffered to be apparent. Plato, who had considered the matter much more deeply than the greater number of orators, asserts positively that in writing an author should always conceal himself, should not allow himself to be remembered, and should put forward only the things and the persons which he wishes to impress upon the reader. See how much more elevated and well-founded were the ideas of those ancient writers than ours.

B: You have told us much regarding the descriptive art: will you now make some observations respecting *action:* of what service is it?

A: To impress upon the mind of the hearer what the speaker wishes.

B: What does this action consist of?

A: Of words, and of gestures of the body.

B: What action can there possibly be in words?

A: Very much indeed. Cicero relates that even the enemies of Gracchus were not able to refrain from weeping when he pronounced these words: " Unhappy that I am! whither shall I go? in what asylum shall I find rest? In the Capitol? it is deluged with the blood of my brother! In my own house? there I shall behold an unhappy mother dissolved in tears and overwhelmed with grief." This is the kind of action I mean. If that were repeated quietly and tamely it would lose all its force.

B: Do you think so?

A : You will think so, too, if you try the experiment. Suppose that I say: " I do not know where to go in my unhappiness; no refuge remains open to me. The Capitol is the spot where the blood of my brother has been spilled: my own house the place where I shall see my mother weeping for grief." This is essentially the same as the other speech. But what has become of that fire and vivacity which was in the words? Where are those half-stifled words which expressed so naturally and so well the transports of grief? The manner in which things are said makes visible the intensity with which they are felt, and that forces the hearer to feel them much more. In those passages, not only are many thoughts not needed, but one may even do without order and coherence in the words: unless this is remembered there is no longer any similarity to passion; and nothing is so unnatural and offensive as to hear passionate sentiments declaimed with pompous language and in measured periods. On that subject I send you back to Longinus: you will see there some marvellous examples out of Demosthenes.

B : I understand all that: but you have made us hope for an explanation of the bodily gestures suitable for oratory, and this I cannot let you pass over.

A : I do not pretend here to deliver an entire course of Rhetoric, if even I were capable of doing so: I only repeat to you certain facts which I have remarked. Action among the Greeks and Romans was much more violent than it is with us: we see this in Cicero and in Quintilian: they used to stamp with the feet, and even give themselves blows on the forehead. Cicero tells a story of an advocate who threw himself upon the client whom he was defending, and tore open his garments in order to show to the judges the wounds which he had received in the service of the Republic. That was a violent action indeed; but such action was reserved for extraordinary occasions. He does not even mention the continual repetition of a gesture. For example, it is not at all natural to be constantly waving the arm while speaking. When one is animated, it is proper to wave the arm; but it is not proper to wave the arm in order to give an appearance of animation. There are even sentiments that it is desirable to utter tranquilly, and without any gesture at all.

B: What! would you wish that a preacher, for example, should not make a gesture occasionally? That would seem very extraordinary.

A: I allow that it is the rule, or at least, the custom, for a preacher to employ action to accompany almost everything he says: but it is easy to show that our preachers often use *too much* action: and that they sometimes also use *too little*.

B: Indeed! please to explain that; for I have

always thought from the example of N., that there should be only two or three kinds of movements of the hands made throughout an entire sermon.

A : Let us come to the principle of the thing. Of what service is a gesture of the body while speaking? Is it not to express the feelings and passions which occupy the soul?

B : I think so.

A : The movement of the body is then a depicting of the thoughts of the mind?

B : Yes.

A : Then that copy ought to be like the original. Everything in it should represent naturally and vividly the sentiments of the speaker, and the nature of the words he speaks. I know, of course, that a low or comic imitation would not be admissible.

B : It seems to me that you are right; and I understand already what you mean. Permit me to interrupt you, in order that I may show you how far I enter into all the consequences of your principles. You would have an orator express by a vigorous, but natural *action* what his words express only in a comparatively feeble manner. Thus, according to your view, the action is really a picture of the thought predominating at the moment in his mind.

A : No doubt. But notice what follows from that: it is, that in order thus to depict in a life-like manner, we must imitate nature, and observe what she does when left unconstrained by art.

B : Yes, I agree to that.

A : Well, then, when merely simple ordinary things are said, unmingled with any deep feeling, would there naturally be many gestures used ?

B : No.

A : It must then be proper not to make any, or to make but few, on similar occasions in public speeches: for everything should be made to accord with nature. Even more, there are subjects on which a speaker will better express his sentiments by a cessation of every movement. If a man, possessed by a lofty sentiment, remains for an instant motionless: that kind of shock holds the very souls of his hearers for a moment in suspense.

B : I understand that those suspenses, well employed, are fine, and touch the hearer powerfully: but it seems to me that you would reduce one who speaks in public to the use of only the same amount of gesture as would be employed by one who was conversing in a private company.

A : Pardon me: the sight of a great assemblage, and the importance of the subject to be treated, ought, without doubt, to animate a preacher to a much greater effort than if he were simply in conversation. But, whether in public or in private, he should always act naturally, so that the body should have movement when the words have stir and energy, and should remain quiet when they are only simple and calm. Nothing seems to me so shocking and absurd as to see a man who frets and excites himself in order to say to me things that are cold and unimpassioned: while he perspires, he makes my blood run absolutely cold. It is some time since I slept at a sermon; but you know that sleep sometimes surprises one during the afternoon sermons: indeed, anciently there was no preaching, except in the morning, after the Gospel in the Liturgy. I soon awaked, and I heard the preacher throwing himself into an extraordinary state of excitement; so that I supposed for a moment that he was treating upon some extremely important point of morality.

B: What was it then?

A: Well, he was only giving notice to his hearers that on the following Sunday he would preach upon penitence. That notice, given with so great an amount of vehemence, surprised me, and would have made me laugh had not respect for the place and the service forbidden it. The greater number of these declaimers use gestures as they use their voice: the one has a perpetual monotony, and the other a uniformity,* which is not less

---
* "It is certain that the adoption of a religious voice in the pulpit, a voice distinct from the ordinary tone, and intended to convey an impression of greater solemnity, is one of the chief causes of the

wearisome, not less far removed from nature, not less detrimental to the good effect which might be expected to follow from action.

B: You asserted also that sometimes they have not *sufficient* action.

A: Is that astonishing? They do not at all

---

preacher being regarded as artificial, and his subject foreign to our ordinary business and our serious worldly interests. No one can tell how much this simple and common blunder has done to sever our religion from our ordinary life, and relegate it to special movements, so as to be assumed with Sunday clothes and services. It should, therefore, be the first duty of a sound rhetorician to extirpate this fatal mannerism in the preacher, and insist that real seriousness is quite inconsistent with any such airs and graces."
—MAHAFFY: *Decay of Modern Preaching,* p. 146.

" A novice among the Jesuits, no matter what he may have been previously—whether a lawyer, author, preacher, canon, grand vicar, bishop, or even a cardinal—must attend a reading-class three or four times a week. There he is made to read like a child, is taught to articulate and accentuate, and every now and then is stopped, while those present are called upon to point out the merits and defects in his reading. This training is persisted in until his pronunciation is perfect, and he is free from all disagreeable accent. But that is not all: every Monday during his noviciate, or during the term of his studies, that is for five, six, eight, or ten years, he has to undergo a training in the tones, which consists in his being made to recite what is called the formula of the general tones—a short discourse, comprising all the tones ordinarily used in oratorical compositions; such as the tone of persuasion, of menace, of kindness, of anger, of the mercy and justice of God, of prayer and of authority. Thereby the young preacher is taught how to supple, to break in his own organisms, and to adapt it to those different tones. After these come the special tones. This consists of a short discourse, to be composed in two hours, on a given text, and must contain certain specified strokes of oratory."—MULLOIS, p. 243.

distinguish the subjects in which it is needful to be animated : they exhaust themselves upon commonplace subjects, and are reduced to say feebly those which require some vehemence of action. It must be confessed that our nation has but little capability for that vehemence; it is too light, and does not take things with sufficient seriousness. The Romans, and still more the Greeks, were admirable in that respect; the Easterns, and particularly the Hebrews, excelled in it. Nothing equals the vivacity and the power, not only of the metaphors which they used in their discourses, but also of the gestures which they employed to express their feelings: as the putting ashes upon their heads, rending their garments, and putting on sackcloth in times of great distress and grief. I do not speak at all of the actions which the prophets did in order to symbolize more vividly the predictions which they made, because they were inspired by God : but without considering things Divinely inspired, we see that those people understood how to express grief, fear, and other passions, in a very different way than that we now employ. Thence came, without doubt, those great effects of eloquence which now are seen no longer.

B : You would wish then for considerable variety in gesture and in the inflections of the voice?

A : It is that which renders action so powerful, and in which Demosthenes is said to have excelled.

The more simple and familiar are the action and the voice in those passages, of which the only object is to instruct, to relate, or explain; the more surprise and emotion are reserved for those other passages in which voice and gesture are raised by a sudden enthusiasm. [Oratory] is a kind of music; and all its beauty consists in the variety of tones which rise or fall according to the nature of the feelings which they are to express.*

B: But if you are right in this matter, even our principal orators are far removed from the perfection of art. The preacher whom we listened to together a fortnight ago did not follow that rule; he did not appear even to try to do so. He said everything in the same tone, the first thirty words excepted; and all the difference there was between the passages in which he wished to be animated, and others, was that in the former he spoke still more rapidly than usual.

A: Pardon me, his voice seemed to have two tones, but they were not at all well adapted to the sense of the words. You are right to say that he

---

* " A man may do good even though he be subject to half-a-dozen drawbacks. Mistakes are often made on this score. One gratification only may suffice to render a man a remarkable orator, whereas another may be free from all obvious defects, and yet be a sorry preacher. The Lord deliver us from a faultless preacher! for he is generally a very bore, as incapable of a trait of genius as he is of a blunder. Always intent on guarding against this and that defect, he loses his personality. He is no longer a man; he is no longer a priest; he is merely a scholar doing his recitation."—MULLOIS, p. 245.

does not follow the rules of inflexion; I think that he has not even felt the need of them. His voice is naturally melodious; but it is very ill-managed, and therefore is not pleasing; as you observed, it did not make any of those touching impressions which it naturally would have done if it had all the inflexions which express the variations of feeling. Such preachers are like fine bells, the sound of which is clear, full, sweet, and agreeable; but after all, are merely bells, which have no meaning, no variety, and on that account no harmony nor eloquence.*

---

* "The modern public is so unused to real rhetoric (as an art) that we set down the vulgarities and failures of rhetoricians as the natural outcome of their science. It must be owing to this strange misapprehension concerning rhetoric, that in our principal divinity schools among Protestants no care is taken to train men in the externals of eloquence, in the proper use of the voice and of the hands, still less in the proper method of constructing a persuasive discourse by an adherence to reasonable rules. . . . Are we to insist that preachers now-a-days are, like the Apostles, to take no heed what they shall say for that the Spirit will give them utterance? For this, too, is a reason why the study of rhetoric is discouraged among religious people. Here we again stand face to face with that very noble but ideal view of the preacher as a man of intense piety, inspired to speak with more than mortal power and wisdom, and trusting implicitly to the Divine Spirit to give him words. Without for one moment denying the existence of such men in all ages of the Church, we may fairly say that to depend on such grounds in ordinary preaching is not only chimerical, but tends to prevent the preacher from adopting the lawful means of persuasion placed within his reach. He might as well start upon a voyage round the world, and expect that the power of strange tongues would be given him to preach to the nations he found on his way."

—J. P. MAHAFFY: *Decay of Modern Preaching*, p. 72.

B : But that rapidity of discourse has nevertheless much beauty of its own.

A : No doubt that is the case: and I agree that in certain vigorous passages it is proper to speak more quickly : but to speak with precipitation, and not to be able to restrain oneself, is a great defect. There are sentiments which need to be supported by a suitable tone of voice and corresponding gesture. It is then with action and voice as it is with verses : sometimes a slow and grave measure is needed for sentiments of that kind, as there is also need sometimes of a short and rushing rhythm of speech to signify ardent and vigorous feelings. To make use always of the same gesture and the same speech of voice would be like one who should give the same remedy to all kinds of sick. But that preacher must be pardoned for his sameness of voice and gesture, for he has many very estimable qualities ; and besides, this defect of his is inevitable in him. Have we not said that the management of the voice should correspond with the sense of the words ? Well, his style is the same all through : it has no variety : on the one side, it has nothing familiar, winning, and popular : on the other, nothing vivid, figurative and sublime : it is a steady stream of words which press one upon the other ; the conclusions are exact, the arguments well maintained and conclusive, the descriptions faithful : in one word, he is a man who speaks in very suitable terms, and who expresses very judicious sentiments. We must even acknowledge that the pulpit is under great obligations to him; he has withdrawn it from slavery to declaimers, and has filled it with much power and dignity. He is very capable of producing conviction: but I know hardly any preacher who has less power of persuading and touching an audience. If you watch him carefully, you will see that he is not even very skilful; for, besides that his manner is neither familiar nor winning, he has, as we have already remarked elsewhere, no tenderness nor warmth. He addresses the understanding only, and the imagination not at all. Now there are arguments which require warmth and intensity of spirit. Scarcely anything which he may have said remains in the memory of those who have listened to him: his discourse is a torrent which suddenly rushes past, and leaves its channel dry. In order to make a durable impression, it is needful to aid the mind by touching the feelings: instructions that are dry and uninteresting can scarcely ever succeed. But what I regard as least natural of all in this preacher, is that he keeps his arms in continual movement, even when there is neither stir nor earnestness in words. For such a style, what would be needed is merely the ordinary conversational gesture; or, conversely to such impetuous action, a style full of vehemence and passionate bursts of feeling would be suitable: or, again, it would be well, as I have said, to render the one less vehement, and the other less monotonous. I conclude that he is a great man; but not in the least an orator. A village mission preacher, who knows how to startle hearers and make them weep, reaches far more nearly the point of eloquence.

B : But what means are there of learning in detail the gestures and inflexions of voice which are natural?

A : I have already mentioned to you that the art of good orators consists wholly in observing what nature does when unrestrained. Do not act, as do those bad orators who always declaim, and never *talk* to their hearers. On the contrary, each hearer should be made to think that you are speaking to him in particular. That is, in fact, the use of natural, familiar, and winning tones. To be natural, they should be always grave and modest: and become sonorous and pathetic only in the passages in which the discourse rises and grows earnest. But do not expect to show forth the feelings by the mere effort of the voice: many people, when they shriek and throw themselves into violent passions, only shock and bewilder their hearers. To succeed in depicting the passions, it is needful to study the movements which they inspire. For example, remark the movements of the eyes, the hands, the motions and postures of the whole body: take careful note of the voice of a person when penetrated with grief, or astonished at the sight of something strange. That is nature displaying itself to you; and you have only to follow it. If you employ art, conceal it so well by imitation, that it may be taken for nature. But to speak truth, it is with orators as it is with poets who write elegies and other impassioned forms of poetry: it is necessary to feel the passion in order to depict it well; art, however exquisite it be, never speaks like the real passion of nature undisguised. Thus you will always be a very imperfect orator, if you are not yourself penetrated with the feelings which you wish to depict and inspire in others.:* and it is not from religious feelings that I say this; I speak simply as an orator.

---

* "Some one has said that 'no faculty of the mind is weak which has heart in it.' Certainly it is true that no faculty is strong which has not heart in it; and whoever addresses men has to learn the lesson. If he speaks of the Gospel, he must feel how glorious that is in itself, and how adapted to man's vast need. This must be the undertone of every sermon; like the golden ground on which the angels of Fra Angelico walk and worship. The conviction of it must be as a sun-gleam, smiting his mind, and quickening to activity all its beauty and all its force. If he has not this, his thought will inevitably be obscure, his feeling dull, his utterance wanting in the elements of power. A deist, a fatalist, a materialist, a sceptic of whatever sort, undertaking as a business to preach the Gospel, will inevitably be like a blind man discoursing on the splendors of light the charming and delicate interplay of colours, or like a deaf man describing oratorios. Every one who loves the Gospel will see that he is speaking theoretically, in the way of imitation from report of others, and not from real and rich experience. So his words will want fire. They will stir no emotion, and touch no heart. They will be like a smile, in which the lips laugh, while the rest of the face is harsh and sullen."—R. S. STORRS, D.D.

B: I quite understand that. But you have spoken of the eyes; have they also an eloquence belonging to them?

A: You might be quite sure that they have. Cicero and all the ancients assure us of the fact. Nothing speaks so eloquently as the countenance; it expresses every passion of the soul, but in the countenance, the eyes have the principal power; a single look at the right time will penetrate to the bottom of the heart.

B: You remind me that the preacher of whom we were speaking usually kept his eyes closed; when you looked at him in front, the effect was unpleasing.

A: Because you feel that he was wanting in one of the elements which should have given life and animation to his discourse.

B: But why does he do that?

A: He is under pressure to continue speaking: and he shuts his eyes, because his memory is working laboriously, and this assists it.

B: I certainly remarked that he was burdened with his discourse: sometimes he even repeated many words in order to regain the thread of it. Those repetitions are disagreeable, and seem like a scholar who has learned his lesson imperfectly: they do injustice to any preacher, even the least gifted.

A: It is not the fault of the preacher, but of the method which he, like so many others, followed. As often as they preach sermons learned by heart, so often will they be liable to that embarrassment.

B: What, would you not have sermons learned by heart to be preached? You could not otherwise have them full of power and precision.

A: I would not prevent preachers from learning by heart discourses on extraordinary occasions, when they would have ample time to prepare themselves well beforehand: yet they should be able to preach without doing this.

B: How then? What you say appears incredible.

A: If I am wrong, I am ready to retract: let us examine the matter without prejudice. What is the principal object of the orator? Have we not seen that it is to persuade? And in order to persuade, did we not say that it was needful to touch and arouse the feelings?

B: Yes, undoubtedly.

A: That manner of preaching is then the best which is the most vigorous and the most touching.

B: That is true: but what do you conclude from that?

A: Which of two orators will have the more vigorous and the more touching manner of preaching, he who learns by heart, or he who speaks without reciting word for word a sermon previously prepared?

B : I maintain that it will be he who has learned his discourse by heart.

A : Wait then : let us state clearly what the question is. On the one hand, I suppose a man who writes down his whole discourse exactly, and learns it by heart to the least word. On the other hand, I suppose another, a man of adequate learning, who fills his mind with his subject, who has considerable facility in speaking (for you would not wish that persons without any ability for it should take upon them this duty); a man, in short, who meditates deeply on all the principles of the subject which he has to treat, and all their various applications; which he arranges in an orderly manner in his mind; who prepares the most expressive words by which he designs to make the subject clearly understood; who sets in order all his proofs; who prepares a certain number of touching examples and similes. That man knows, without doubt, all that he ought to say, and the order in which he ought to treat each part of his subject; nothing remains for him to do but to find the familiar expressions which are to make up the body of his discourse. Do you suppose that such a man as that would have any difficulty in finding them?

B : Those that he will find will not be so exact

and so graceful as if he had sought them at his leisure in his study.*

A: Perhaps so. But according to your own showing he will lose nothing but a little ornament; and you know what, according to the principles which we have already laid down, we ought to think of such a loss as that. On the other side, what will he not gain in force and liberty of action, which is the chief thing? Supposing that he is thoroughly skilled in composition, as Cicero declares to be necessary; that he has read all the best

---

* In the same sense a defender of the written sermon argues: " *(a)* In extemporaneous preaching there are many errors in language which mar the beauty and power of the sermon, so that, in the presence of an educated audience, it can not have the force of a well written composition. *(b)* Off-hand preaching is full of inaccuracies of statement, misquotations, and fanciful rhetoric which adds to the distrust, which a want of elegant language has already made. *(c)* There can never be that consistent and systematic handling of a subject by the extemporaneous speaker, which would be possible to him in the deliberate preparations of a written sermon. This off-hand preaching is like off-hand shooting, very liable to miss the mark. *(d)* Extemporaneous preaching is generally addressed to the passions rather than the judgments of men. And the impressions made are like the running of a wet weather spring which soon dries away. Impressions made under excitement, and in the haste of an unguarded moment, are wanting in that solidity which characterizes the changes which are wrought out by clear, well-defined principles. *(e)* The manuscript preacher 'does all things in decency and in order,' as saith the Scripture, 1 Cor. xiv. 40. He appeals with enlightened judgment and chosen language to the spiritual nature of man. He beautifies and adorns known facts with correct language, and points the soul to the blissful home above with words and sentiment culled from the broad fields of Christian literature

models;* that he has much natural and acquired facility; that he has an abundant stock of principles and of learning; that he has well thought out every part of his subject, and arranged it in his mind; we have a right to conclude that he will speak with power, with consecutiveness, and with fulness. His periods will not delight the ear so much, and that will be an advantage; he will be the better orator for that. His transitions from one part of the subject to the other will not be so elegant. That, however, will not be a matter of great consequence. He may, indeed, have prepared these without learning them by heart; but putting that aside, these negligences will be common to him as

---

in which the 'precious promises' shine with a glory which God has given them."—JOHN A. WILLIAMS, D.D.

* "The Bible and the sermons of Chillingworth and Butler were Webster's models. Pitt, when asked the secret of his lofty style, pointed to a volume of Barrow's sermons. The Addisonians were students of Tillotson. Said Dugald Stewart: 'There is a living writer who combines the beauties of Johnson, Addison, and Burke, without their imperfections—Rev. Robert Hall.' Jeremy Taylor is another of the masters. Beecher tells us that Hooker's English was one of his ideals. 'Hooker's elaborate sentence, like the sentences of Demosthenes, composed of parts so hinged, of clauses so subordinated to the main thought, that we foresee the end from the beginning, and close the period with a sense of perfect roundness and totality,' was the model of the most sublime eloquence the world has heard since Demosthenes. Talmage acknowledges Ruskin as his literary and linguistic mentor. However open to criticism Macaulay may be in the choice of words, propriety of phrase, and rhythm of sentence, nevertheless for pervading power, lucidity, coherence, and dramatic progress he stands almost alone."—REV. J. M. DRIVER.

with the most eloquent orators of antiquity, who have thought it advisable thus often to imitate nature and not to betray too elaborate a preparation. In what then will he be wanting? He will make various little repetitions; but they will not be useless. Not only will the hearer, who has good taste, take pleasure in this touch of nature, for it is natural to return again and again to that which is striking in a subject; but this repetition will impress truths more strongly; it is the surest and safest method of instruction. What then? Suppose that you do find in his discourse some construction hardly exact, some term not quite suitable, or not approved by the Academy; something irregular, or even weak or misapplied; which will have escaped from the speaker in the warmth of his oration? A person must have a very small intellect to imagine that such faults are great. Such faults may be found in the most approved authors. The most skilful among the ancients thought nothing of them. If we had as broad views as they we should not occupy ourselves at all with those *minutiæ*. It is only petty grammarians, people who are not qualified to appreciate great things, who amuse themselves with such trifles as these. Pardon my freedom: it is only because I am quite sure that you think very differently from people of that kind, that I speak to you about the matter so frankly.

B: Pray do not measure your words in the

least with me; but come to your conclusion without hesitation.

A : Consider then, in the next place, the advantages of a man who does *not* commit his discourse to memory. He has complete self-possession, he expresses himself in an easy and unaffected way, he does not adopt a declamatory tone; his thoughts flow freely, his expressions (if his natural endowments are well adapted for eloquence) are forcible and full of energy; even the warmth which animates him enables him to find expressions and metaphors which he would not have been able to elaborate in his study.

B : Why? A man may be animated in his study, and may compose very vigorous discourses.

A : That is true: but the warmth of speaking enables him to go in much greater vivacity. Farther, that which comes from the warmth of speaking is altogether natural and acceptable; it has an unstudied air, and has none of the artificial look which belongs to almost all discourses composed at leisure.* Then a skilful and experienced

---

* "The system of preaching lives upon the value of the personal element in it. There is truth enough in the countless volumes of homilies already encumbering our libraries. There is, too, abundant instruction in the ceaseless issues of the religious press. Yet our churches are as well filled as in any previous age, because the people are interested to catch the momentary thoughts and feelings of a living man. It is the personality which makes the sermon. But for this very reason the demand is for genuineness and heartiness in him who

orator adapts his utterances to the impression which they seem to be producing on the hearer: for he watches closely which of these enters, and which does not enter, into their minds, what attracts their attention and touches their hearts, and what produces no effect upon them. The latter he repeats in another form, reclothing it with images and comparisons more familiar and engaging: or he even rises to the principles which are the sources of those truths he is enforcing; or strives to remove the feelings which prevent those truths from making a due impression. This is the true art of instruction and persuasion: without these methods only vague and unfruitful discourses can be preached. See how far the orator, who speaks only what he has learned by heart, is from attaining this degree of success. Set before your mind a man who dares say nothing but what is in the lesson he has committed to memory: all is necessarily dependent upon the style of his discourse; and it will come to be the case with him, as Dionysius of Halicarnassus remarks that it did with Isocrates, that his composition is better

---

speaks. He must be visible. He must have latent heroism. He must have capacity for enthusiasm and the courage of his convictions. When the preacher appears in the pulpit, therefore, he must not exhibit himself as a student, though he needs thorough scholarship; he must not wear the manner of an ecclesiastic, though he may be in very deed a priest dealing with things pertaining to God; he must not seem to have come from the covert of a recluse, though he may have gained power from solitary communings with God."—E. G. SELDEN.

adapted to be read than to be delivered by word of mouth. Besides, let him do what he will, his inflexions of voice will be monotonous and always a little forced; he is not a man speaking, but an orator reciting or declaiming: his action is at random, his eyes too fixed show the labour of his memory, and he dare not yield himself to any extraordinary impulse or emotion, without incurring the danger of losing the thread of his discourse. The hearer, seeing the artifice, which is so evident, is far from being interested and carried out of himself, as he should be; but on the contrary, watches coldly and critically the whole method and contrivance of the discourse.

B: But did not the ancient orators do that which you condemn?

A: I believe not.

B: What! do you suppose that Demosthenes and Cicero did not know by heart those harangues, so finished and so polished, which we have of theirs?

A: We see, of course, that they committed them to writing: but we have many reasons for believing that they did not commit them to memory word for word. In fact, the discourses of Demosthenes, such as we have them now in a written form, bear much clearer signs of the vehemence and loftiness of a great genius accustomed to speak strongly on public affairs, than of the exactitude and polish of an author who is composing an oration before delivering it. As for Cicero, there are to be seen, in various passages of his Orations, sentences adapted to incidents that happened at the moment, and which could not possibly, therefore, have been prepared previously. But let us take his own statement upon that matter. He thinks that an orator should have a good memory. He even speaks of *artificial memory* as a useful invention: but nothing that he has said goes so far as to lay down that a discourse should be learned by heart to the last word. On the contrary, he appears to limit himself to the wish that a speaker should arrange in his mind all the parts of his discourse, that he should prepare beforehand all the illustrations and principal expressions that he ought to use, reserving, however, the power to add at the moment what the sight of the audience may suggest, or what need may require to be said; it is for this reason that he is express in demanding so much care and presence of mind in the orator.*

---

* "If by extempore sermons you mean those delivered without manuscript, I believe them to be, speaking generally, the sermons of the future. In the sense of being produced on the spur of the moment, very few sermons are, and none ought to be, extempore. But preaching without manuscript has, in my opinion, formed a very material element in the past success of dissent. There is a *primâ facie* reality about it which is rarely communicated to discourses delivered from writing. The Church is very seriously handicapped so long as the majority of the clergy are tied to their sermon-books. This seems to be more and more admitted, with the probable result that the coming generation will, in the main, leave their sermon-books behind them."

—TWELLS, *Colloquies*, p. 153.

B: Permit me to say that I am not in the least convinced by all that: I cannot believe that anyone can speak so well, without having weighed every word that he utters.

C: For my part, I can well understand what renders you so incredulous: you judge of this matter by common experience. If people who are in the general habit of learning their sermons by heart should perchance preach without that preparation, they would evidently preach very badly. I am not astonished at that: for they are not accustomed to throw themselves upon the natural powers of speech: their efforts have been directed only towards learning to write, and, moreover, to write with this particular intention: they have never thought of learning to speak in a manner noble, strong, and natural. Furthermore, the greater number have not a sufficient foundation of doctrinal knowledge to be able to trust themselves to their own resources in the pulpit. The method of learning by heart puts a certain number of persons who have but narrow and superficial minds in a condition to deliver public discourses with some credit; all that they need do is to collect a sufficient store of thoughts and quotations from the writings of others, and combine these: and, however small be their genius and constructive power, they can, *in time*, give a polished and regular form to that material. But, for the other method, is needed a serious consideration of the first principles of

Religion, an extensive knowledge of character, some reading in ancient authors, with a power of reasoning and of action. Is not that what you think requisite for an orator who dispenses with learning his discourse by heart?*

A: You have stated it very well. Only it may not be superfluous to add that even when the qualities which this method requires are not found in any marked degree in a man, he may nevertheless

---

* Here is a brief summing up of the entire question: "There are some who ought not to use written sermons ordinarily. They have the off-hand instinct. They take fire in presence of an audience. The 'nimble servitors' are never found off duty. Thought crystallizes, for them, into richer forms in the pulpit than in the study. The mechanism of their minds is adjusted to extemporaneous work. They have the temperament in which the requisite elements are mingled with fulness of all and waste of none. There are others who can work most effectively when their hand grips the pen. They can penetrate deeper. They can see more clearly. They can gain broader outlook. The work of clothing their thought in words worthy of being reduced to record reacts to clarify and intensify and liberalize the thought. They can use a manuscript in the pulpit with effectiveness. They can speak more forcibly because of the aid which it gives. They can read without reading. They are not exposed to the peril of repeating themselves. They have no need to hesitate between different forms of expression; the question of preference has been carefully considered and settled. The instinctive feeling that they are not quite sure of saying what they desire, and as they desire, is not interfering with the free play of their powers. They are not dependent on the presence of an audience for an enkindling of the intellectual and emotional fires of their nature. Tears drop on the sheets as they are covering them. Underneath the sentences are unrecorded prayers. The spaces between the lines are replete with thanksgiving and hope."—REV. S. C. LEONARD.

succeed in making good discourses, provided that he has a fair degree of mental power, a reasonable stock of knowledge, and some facility in speaking. In this method, as in the other, there will be various ranks of orators. Take notice also, that the greater number of those who speak without learning by heart do not prepare sufficiently :* it is really necessary for them to study their subject with the closest attention, to prepare all the passages by which they hope to touch and impress their audience: and to arrange all in order which may be of use in helping them to recall all parts of their subject again, in their proper connexion.

B: You have already frequently mentioned that *order:* do you mean anything else than a division? Have you upon that subject also some peculiar opinion?

A: You are, as you think, speaking in jest: but the fact is, that I am not less singular in my opinion on that subject than on the others.

B: Are you really serious?

---

* "That the sermon ought to be thoroughly prepared, whether the one or the other method is adopted, is a truism. A mushroom cannot be transformed into a shock of corn fully ripe by any method of gathering it. Writing is as indispensable to the improvisator as to the pastor who has a manuscript back of his sermon. The pen ought to be in daily use by the pastor, whatever method he adopts of 'attaching truth to the life of his people.' Writing is one of the conditions of his mental health. He needs to write in order to do unwritten work. He needs to write in order to understand himself."—REV. S. C. LEONARD.

A : Be assured that I am : and since we are on the subject, I am going to show you how defective is the *order* adopted by the greater number of orators.

B : Since you love order so much, *divisions* ought not to displease you.

A : But I am far from approving of them.

B : Why? Do they not render a discourse orderly and methodical?

A : Frequently, and indeed generally, they are put where they should not properly be, and thus they hinder a discourse, and render it uninteresting. They cut it up into two or three parts, which interrupts the action of the orator, and hinders the effect which it ought to produce. There is no longer a true unity in the discourse : it is divided into two or three different discourses, which are united only by an arbitrary bond. The sermon of the day before yesterday, that of yesterday, and that of to-day, provided that they are according to a plan strictly followed out, like the plans of sermons for Advent, make up just as much the body of a single discourse as the three points of one of those sermons make up together one sermon.

B : But what is order then, according to your views? What confusion there would be in a discourse which was not divided at all !*

---

* "When a sermon is mainly didactic, when it consists of a series of motives to enforce some duty, or of a carefully organized procession of

A : Do you suppose that there was much more confusion in the harangues of Demosthenes and of Cicero, than in the sermons of the preacher of your parish?

B : I do not know: I suppose not.

A : Do not be afraid to concede too much: the harangues of those great men are not divided as are the sermons of the present time. Not only they, but also Isocrates, of whom we have said so much, and the other ancient orators never

---

proofs in support of some doctrinal or ethical proposition, the announcement of the divisions will probably help your congregation to understand and to remember what you are saying. But I see no more reason for always announcing the divisions of a sermon than for always announcing the divisions of a speech. If the thoughts of the sermon are well massed, if land and water, earth and sky, are definitely separated from each other, instead of being left in the confusion of chaos, the sermon will be effective at the time, and the main points of it will be remembered afterwards, whether the divisions are announced or not. There are some obvious disadvantages in announcing them. The sermon is in danger of becoming a series of short sermons, with the divisions for separate texts; and there is sometimes a great deal of trouble in making a natural and easy transition from one division to another. . . . This method has the advantage of stimulating and suspending curiosity. When the preacher begins by announcing the proposition which he intends to prove or to illustrate, the congregation will generally see a straight piece of road before them, and will feel that their attention may be relaxed till the next turn comes. Sometimes, however, the proposition will be misunderstood, sometimes it will provoke antagonism. The misunderstanding will be obviated if the misunderstanding comes first and the proposition afterwards; and if the proof is given before the proposition is stated, the antagonism may not arise."—R. W. DALE: *Lectures on Preaching*, p. 139.

adopted that method of division at all. The Fathers of the Church did not even know of it. S. Bernard, the last of them, often marks divisions; but he does not follow them, nor does he formally divide his sermons at all. Preaching existed for a long while without sermons having been divided; and it is a very modern invention which comes to us from the scholastic divines.

B: I allow that the schoolmen are but a faulty model for eloquence; but what form was there then anciently given to a discourse?

A: I am about to tell you that. A discourse was not formally divided at all: but all the subjects which it was necessary to distinguish from each other were carefully taken in succession, its own place was assigned to each, and each subject was arranged in proper order, so that it should follow where it would be most likely to make an impression upon the hearer.* Often a consideration which, if

---

* "It is indispensable, therefore, that the main plan of the sermon be from the start so plainly in view that it comes up of itself, as it is needed, and does not require to be pulled into sight with any effort. To this end it must be simple, obvious, natural, so that it fixes itself in the mind; and must be clearly articulated in its parts. If possible, let it be so arranged that one point leads to another, and when the treatment of it is finished, leaves you in front of that which comes next. Then take up that, and treat it in its order until, through that treatment, you reach the third, and find it inevitable to proceed to consider that. By such a progressive arrangement of thought you are yourself carried forward; your faculties have continual liberty; you are not forced to pause in the work of addressing yourself directly to the people."—R. S. STORRS, D.D.

put forth at first, would have appeared of little importance, becomes decisive when it is reserved for the time when the hearer shall have been prepared by other reasonings to appreciate all the power of it. Often a single word, happily employed in the place to which it belongs and which suits it, brings out an entire truth in all its clearness. Sometimes it is needful to leave a truth veiled and disguised till the very end of the speech: it is Cicero who asserts this. In every case there ought to be an orderly succession of proofs; the first should prepare the way for the second, and the second should strengthen the first. It is needful to give a general view of the whole subject to begin with, and to dispose the mind of the hearer favourably towards it, by a modest and winning opening, by order of probity and candour. Then the preacher should go on to lay down his *general principles;* after that to state the *facts* he is engaged upon in a simple, clear, and telling manner, laying special stress upon those of which he means to make use afterwards. First *principles;* then *facts;* and from these draw the *conclusions* which you desire to reach; taking care to arrange the reasoning in such a manner as that the proofs will admit of being borne in mind easily.* All this ought to be done

---

* "The introduction should be as brief as possible. As a rule it should spring directly and naturally out of the text; that is, if the text is announced first. If you want to say something before you refer to your text, keep back your text till you have said it. But the best

in such a manner that the discourse should be continually growing; and that the hearer should feel more and more the growing weight of truth. Then is the time to throw out vivid and striking metaphors, and transitions of rhetoric calculated to excite the feelings. For that purpose it is needful to be acquainted with the interconnections of the feelings; to know which of them may be aroused most easily at first, and may then serve to arouse the others; and finally, which of them are able to produce the greatest effects; for with these latter the discourse should be brought to a close. It is often useful to make at the end a recapitulation or summary, which gathers up in a few sentences all

---

advice I can give you is to get to work as soon as you can. If your text requires explanation, explain it; if not, do not waste your time by explaining it. The time which most young preachers devote to the introduction would be far better spent on the close, or what our fathers used to call the 'Application' of their sermons. About this all our authorities are agreed. An English preacher of the last generation used to say that he cared very little what he said the first half hour, but that he cared a very great deal what he said the last fifteen minutes. I remember reading many years ago an address delivered by Mr. Henry Ward Beecher, in which he gave a very striking account of the sermons of Jonathan Edwards. Mr. Beecher said that in the elaborate doctrinal part of Jonathan Edwards' sermons the great preacher was only getting his guns into position; but that in his 'Application' he opened fire upon the enemy. There are too many of us, I am afraid, who take so much time in getting our guns 'into position,' that we have to finish without firing a shot. We say that we leave the truth to do its own work. We trust to the hearts and consciences of our hearers to 'apply it.' Depend upon it, gentlemen, this is a great and fatal mistake."

—DALE : *Lectures*, p. 145.

the power of the orator, and sets anew before the hearers all that he has said which is most winning and persuasive. At the same time, it is not absolutely necessary always to follow that order in an uniform manner; each subject has its fitnesses and its exceptions. But even in this order a variety may be found almost infinite. This method, which is almost marked out for us by Cicero, cannot, as you see, be followed in a discourse which is cut invariably into three parts, nor observed absolutely in every point. An order is needful, but not an order that is expressly stated and shown from the commencement of the discourse. Cicero says that the best course, almost always, is to conceal it; and to lead on the hearer without his perceiving it. He goes so far as to state distinctly (I remember it well) that a speaker ought to conceal even the number of his arguments, so that they may not be counted, although they may be distinct in themselves, and in his own mind: and that a discourse ought *not* to have any clearly marked divisions. But the lack of discernment of late has gone so far that people do not recognize at all the order of a discourse, unless the speaker warns them of it at the commencement, and makes a pause at each point.*

---

* "It is not always best, I think, to have the frame of a sermon like the frame of a Swiss cottage, all shown on the outside. It may be better to keep it within, and to have the presence and the strength of it manifested only in the dignity and stability of the structure which it braces and governs. But it must be there, and give symmetry and security to all the details which grow up upon it."—R. S. STORRS, D.D.

C: But do not divisions serve as an assistance to the mind and memory of the hearer? It is for this practical purpose they are made.

A: Divisions help the memory of the *speaker*. But the observance of a natural and consecutive order in subjects would effect that object still better, and that without being specially marked: since the true connexion of subjects best guides the mind. But as for divisions, the only people whom they help are those who have studied it, and whom their course of instruction has rendered familiar with that method; and if the great body of hearers remember the divisions better than the rest of the discourse, it is because they have been repeated more frequently. Generally speaking, things which are plain and practical will be best remembered.

B: The order which you propose may be good for certain subjects, but it is not suitable for all; it is not always the case that there are facts to be made landmarks of.

A: When there are none such we must do without them; but there are scarcely any subjects in which they are wanting. One of the excellences of Plato is that he is in the habit of setting down, at the commencement of his treatises on morals, the histories and traditions which form, so to speak, the foundation of the rest of the discourse. That method is still more suitable to those who are preaching sermons; since Religion is entirely founded on antiquity, on history, on tradition. The greater number of preachers do not give sufficient instruction in their sermons; and because they do not go back to those original sources [of Religion] their proofs of it are but weak.

B: You have already been speaking to us for a long time, and I am ashamed to delay you still more; but curiosity obliges me. Permit me, then, to ask you some farther questions respecting the rules to be observed in discourses.

A: Willingly; I am not yet wearied, and I have still a little time to devote to conversation.

B: You would strictly exclude from discourses all frivolous ornaments: now would you show me, by some plain examples, how to distinguish between such paste jewels (so to speak) and those which are solid and natural?

A: Have you any liking for *trills* in music? Do you not prefer those stirring tones which are descriptive of facts, and which express the feelings?

B: Yes, undoubtedly. Trills and quavers do nothing but amuse the ear: they mean nothing, and express no feeling. At one time our music was full of them: and then its general character was feeble and confused. At the present time we are beginning to make some return to the music of an earlier period. That music was a kind of impassioned declamation: and it acts powerfully on the mind.

A : I am sure that music, of which you are so good a judge, would assist me to make the matter in hand, which relates to eloquence, clear to you. And there should be a kind of eloquence even in music: *trills* should be rejected in eloquence as well as in music. Do you not understand now what it is that I call *trills* in discourse—a succession of similar and monotonous periods, which continually return like refrains; a sort of *humming (bourdonnement)* of words which return perpetually like the burden of a song? That is false eloquence, which resembles music in bad taste.

B : But still, make that yet a little more plain and clear to me.

A : The reading of good orators and of bad ones will form your taste more certainly than all rules: nevertheless, it is easy to satisfy you by bringing forward some examples. I will not take any from our own time, although it is fertile in instances of false ornament. Let us, in order not to wound anyone, return to Isocrates; especially as he is the model of those flowery and pompous discourses which are now the fashion. Have you read that eulogy of Helen which is so much admired?

B : Yes, I once read it.

A : What opinion did you form of it?

B: I thought it admirable: I have never read a composition displaying so much genius, eloquence, sweetness, fancy and tenderness. I confess to you that Homer, whom I read afterwards, did not appear to me to have in any degree the same power of genius. But just now, that you have pointed out to me the true object of poets and orators, I see clearly that Homer greatly surpasses Isocrates in as much as his art is concealed, while that of the other is visible and purposely displayed. But still, I was charmed with Isocrates at that time, and I should be still if you had not opened my eyes. M—— is the Isocrates of our time; and I see clearly that, in pointing out the weakness of that orator, you are arraigning all those who try to imitate that flowery and effeminate eloquence.

A: I speak now only of Isocrates. In the commencement of that eulogy he brings forward the love which Theseus had had for Helen, and he imagines that he will give an exalted idea of that lady by depicting the heroic qualities of that great man who was so passionately attached to her: as if Theseus, whom antiquity has always described as feeble and inconstant in his attachments, could not possibly have been attracted by any woman, but one of surpassing charms. Then he comes to the judgment of Paris. Juno, he says, promised to him the Empire of Asia, Minerva, victory in war, and Venus, the beautiful Helen. Then he goes on to say, that as Paris was not able, in that judgment, to gaze upon the faces of those goddesses because of the lustre which shone from them, he could only form his judgment from the value of the three prizes which were offered to him: and he preferred Helen to an Empire and to victory. Then he praises the judgment of him to whose discernment even goddesses submitted themselves. "I am astonished,"* he says, again in favour of Paris, "that anyone should regard him as ill-judging in deciding to live with her, on whose account so many demi-gods were willing to die."

C: I can imagine that I hear the preachers of our day indulging in antitheses and epigrams. There is a good deal of Isocrates in many of them!

A: Here is their master. All the rest of that eulogy is full of the same peculiarities; he is greatly occupied with the long war of Troy, with the evils which the Greeks suffered in order to recover Helen by force, and with the praise of that beauty which is so powerful over men. Nothing at all is taken in a serious spirit; not one truth of morals is brought out in the course of all this; he judges of the value of things only by the violent passions of men. And not only are his arguments feeble, his style is also weak and overloaded with ornament. I have reminded you of that passage, although it

---

* Θαυμάζω δ'εἴ τὶς ὄιεται κάκως βεβούλευσθαι τοὺ μετὰ ταύτης ζῆν ἑλόμενον, ἧς ἕνεκα πόλλοι των ἡμιθέων ἀποθνῄσκειν ἠθέλησαν.

is so objectionable, because it is very much praised, and because that faulty style is now very much imitated. The other and more serious orations of Isocrates show much of that effeminacy of style, and are full of those false jewels of rhetoric.

B : I see very clearly that you will have nothing to do with those clever terms of phrase which are neither solid and conclusive arguments, nor the expression of natural and tender impulses. Even the example from Isocrates, which you bring forward, although it is on a frivolous subject, does not fail to be convincing; and all that tinsel is still less becoming to serious and grave subjects.

A : Let us return to Isocrates. Am I wrong in speaking of that orator as Cicero assures us Aristotle spoke of him?

B : What has Cicero said?

A : That Aristotle, seeing that Isocrates had turned the eloquence of tone and gesture to the purposes of displaying and amusement, and was drawing after him many imitators, applied to him a verse from the "Philoctetes," in order to show how much he was ashamed to be silent and listen to that declaimer. But now enough of this matter; it is necessary that I should leave you.

B : Pray stay for a moment yet. Do you not then admit any antitheses at all?

A : Pardon me: when subjects naturally opposed the one to the other are touched upon, it is quite right to emphasize their opposition. Antithesis is then the briefest and most simple manner of explaining the true nature of things; it is natural, and has, without doubt, a real beauty of its own. But to make a circuitous preparation in order to explode a sort of battery of words is puerile. At first people of bad taste are dazzled; but presently those affectations weary the hearer. Do you know the architecture of our old churches, which is called Gothic?

B: Yes, I know it; it is seen everywhere.

A: Have you not remarked those roses, those projections, those litttle irregular carved ornaments; in short, all those gewgaws of which it is full? They are in architecture what antitheses and the other plays upon words are in eloquence. Greek architecture is much more simple: it admits only dignified and natural ornaments. In it you see nothing but what is grand, regular, and in proportion. The architecture which is called Gothic came to us from the Arabs. That race of people, being very full of impulse, and without discipline and culture, could not help devoting themselves to such false refinements; and out of that tendency came bad taste in all other departments. They became sophistical in reasoning, lovers of gewgaws in architecture, and inventors of phrases and witticisms in poetry and in eloquence. All of these belong to the same class of mind.

B : That is very amusing. According to you, a sermon full of antitheses and similar ornamentations is like a church built in the Gothic style.

A : Precisely.

B : Just one more question, I beg of you, and then I will let you go.

A : What is it?

B : It seems to me that it is very difficult to treat details in a dignified style; yet that is necessary when we wish to be sound, natural, and unaffected in diction, as you require. Be so kind as to say a word on this subject also.

A : In our nation there is so much apprehension of being undignified, because the expressions used, as a general rule, are plain, bold, and indefinite. If anyone wishes to praise a saint, he seeks out magnificent phrases; he declares that the object of his praise was admirable, that his virtues were heavenly, that he was rather an angel than a man; and all this he says in a series of exclamations, without connection or graphic power. The Greeks, on the contrary, made little use of all these general terms, which prove nothing, but brought forward great numbers of facts. For example, Xenophon, in the whole of his Cyropædia, does not say once that Cyrus was admirable; yet he makes him everywhere to be admired. It is thus that it is proper to praise the saints by exhibiting their sentiments and their actions in detail. We have, in this respect, a false politeness very similar to that of certain people from the provinces who pride themselves on their good breeding : they do not dare to use any expression which does not appear to them to be elegant and refined ; thus they are always stiff and high-flown, and think that they would let themselves down too much if they called things by their proper names.* Eloquence ought to

---

* " If [persons] are to speak at all, let 'em speak out. Persons beat about the bush until you quite lose sight of 'em, ay, and the bush too."
—TWELLS : *Colloquies*, p. 197.

"I do not know how far, in the country districts and in the quieter towns, the educated feeling has let go of religion as it has been hitherto taught in the churches, but I am confident that in our larger cities and centres, and particularly in circles of artists, of scientists, and of literary men, there is an essential unclasping of the mind in this respect; and we hear thousands of men saying, 'The pulpit has had its day; these old-fashioned doctrines have no more juice in them ; and according to the great principle of evolution, we have so far grown that at last the whole world is becoming man's text-book, and the minister ought to preach to his people the great elements of physical life and health, the great sociological laws, the great civil laws, and the great laws of political economy.' In short, there are many men who would teach you that now, in the light that has been growing through the ages, the time has come when science is to be the saviour of the world, that the minister should be its instrument, and that the pulpit should be the place where it is taught, in its relations to life and duty. Far be it from me to undervalue science, which I believe to be one of the revelations of God in this world. The heavens declare His glory, and the earth shows His handiwork ; and if rightly understood and reverently observed, they lead us back to God ; but physical science has not in it the power to develop spirituality in man. When taught only upon this lower plane of knowledge—namely, the knowledge which they can see, and hear,

be able to treat upon every subject. Even poetry, which is the most elevated kind of speech, is only successful when it depicts things with all their circumstances. See Virgil, when he represents the Trojan ships leaving the coast of Africa, or arriving on that of Italy; every detail is to be found in his poem. But it must be confessed that the Greeks pushed detail much further still, and followed nature very closely indeed. On account of this multiplicity of details many people would say, if they dared, that Homer was too plain and simple in his narrative. By this strongly marked simplicity, for which we have too much lost the taste at the present day, this poet resembles the Scriptures in a considerable degree; but the Scriptures surpass him as much as they have surpassed all the rest of antiquity in depicting events naturally and artlessly. When detail is being described nothing should be presented to the mind of the hearer which does not merit his attention, and which does not contribute to the impression which it is desired to make upon him. It is necessary to be judicious in the choice of the circumstances to be described, but no hesitation ought to be felt in using any word which serves to

---

and smell, and taste, and handle—men can never become spiritual. . . . As an auxiliary, material science is invaluable, but it touches man only in the lower sphere of life, and never exalts him into that higher realm upon which he may enter as a Christian."

—H. W. BEECHER: *Lectures on Preaching, Third Series*, p. 3.

describe them. It is a mistaken politeness to suppress certain useful details because they are not found capable of being presented in an ornamental way. Besides this, Homer teaches us sufficiently, by his example, that it is possible to embellish all subjects in a way appropriate to each. Nevertheless, it must be understood that every discourse ought to have its light and shade; it is proper to be dignified in speaking of great things; to be simple, without being low, when treating of little things; sometimes artlessness and liberality is needful, sometimes sublimity and passion. A painter who only represented palaces of sumptuous architecture would not be true to nature, and would soon weary the beholder. Nature must be followed in her contrasts: after having depicted a stately town, it is often advisable to put before the spectator a desert and the huts of shepherds.* Most people, who wish to make a fine discourse, try to employ a pomp of words indis-

---

* The quintessence of plainness and homeliness is the proverb. Of the use of these in the pulpit an American writer says: " The proverb is the concentration and crystallization into the smallest compass, of universal truths—the ' wisdom which knows neither language or race.' Often a nation's history is contained in a single sentence, a volume of wisdom in a single line, an age-long, world-wide truth in a single word. Our Saviour strung these glittering gems upon the threads of His discourses. The whole Bible scintillates like a diamond-bank, with these undated, cosmopolitan coins. To digest a proverb each day would, in a single year, transform our sounding brass and tinkling cymbals into discourses of gold."—REV. J. M. DRIVER.

criminately in all parts of it: they think they have done everything necessary when they have drawn together a mass of sounding words and vague sentiments: their sole object is to load their discourses with ornament: in this they are like to unskilful cooks, who do not know how to observe moderation in seasoning, and think that they have given an exquisite flavour to viands, when they have heaped them with salt and pepper. True eloquence is in no way ambitious or ostentatious; it is restrained, and always adapted and proportioned to the people addressed and the subjects treated of: it is grand and sublime only when it is needful so to be.

B : The mention that you made just now of the Holy Scripture has made me extremely desirous that you would enable me too to appreciate intelligently its beauty : shall we not have that pleasure at some hour to-morrow ?

A : It will be difficult for me to come to-morrow: but I will try to do so this evening. Since you wish it, we will speak then of the word of God; hitherto we have spoken only of the words of men.

B : Adieu, then, sir; I beg you not to fail us. If you do not appear, we shall come to look for you.

Third Dialogue.

True Eloquence: in what it consists. How admirable is that of the Sacred Scripture. The importance of Holy Scripture, and the right manner of explaining it. The means of training oneself for preaching. What ought to be the chief matter of instructions. On the eloquence of the Fathers, and their style. On panegyrics.

C: I was beginning to fear that you would not come: and I had almost gone to M.'s house to look for you.

A: A matter of business detained me: but happily I was able to get through it.

C: I am very glad of that: for we are most desirous to go on with the subject entered upon this morning.

B: After I left you, I was at a sermon at . . . and I thought of you. The preacher spoke in a very edifying manner: but I doubt if the people quite understood what he said.

A: That too often happens. I once heard an ingenious lady observe that preachers speak Latin in French. The most essential quality of a preacher is to be instructive. But in order to instruct others it is necessary to be well instructed oneself.*

---

* "The minister is a physician of a far higher order. He has a vast field before him. He has to study an infinite variety of constitutions. He is to furnish himself with the knowledge of the whole system of remedies. He is to be a man of skill, and expedient. If one thing fail, he must know how to apply another. Many intricate and perplexed cases will come before him; it will be disgraceful to him not to be prepared for such. His patients will put many questions to him; it will be disgraceful to him not to be prepared to answer them. He is a merchant embarking in extensive concerns. A little ready money in the pocket will not answer the demands that will be made upon him. Some of us think it will, but they are grossly deceived. There must be a well-furnished account at the banker's. . . . Knowledge, then, and truth, are to be the constant aim of a young minister. But where shall we find them? Let him learn from a fool, if a fool can teach him anything; let him be everywhere and always a learner."

—CECIL : *Remains*, p. 159.

"In writing sermons, nothing can be done by the minister without *knowledge*. There can be no substitute for this—all rules and principles to be observed in such compositions are worthless without it. It is vain to talk about the mint, till you have secured the bullion. Therefore I suggested to you a scheme of reading before I ventured upon any hints about sermons—'Reading makes the full man'; and surely if a full man is wanted anywhere, it is in the minister of a church who is fixed to the same spot the whole year round; and who has to produce himself from week to week before the same audience. Nothing short of a large magazine to draw upon will suffice for these frequent demands—without it, the thread of his speech will soon run out the staple of his argument; and instead of a preacher he will become a spin-text. This should be looked to by us. It is unfair to exact the attention of an audience for a considerable time, and supply them ourselves with nothing to fix it. It is unfair to charge them with indifference, lukewarmness, and irreligion, when they are merely weary of listening to one who cannot teach because he will not learn—they have no option but to hear—they are in the condition of animals long tethered upon a bare pasture, they cannot escape, but you must not be

On the one hand, it is needful to appreciate fully the meaning of what the Scriptures say : on the other, to be acquainted with the precise mental range of the minds we are addressing. That requires first, a solid basis of knowledge ; and secondly, great discernment. We speak constantly to the people of the Scriptures, of the Church, of the two Laws, of the sacrifices, of Moses, Aaron, Melchisedek ; of the Prophets and the Apostles ; and yet we do not give ourselves the least trouble to teach them what all these things mean, and what all these holy persons have done. A person may follow some preachers continually for twenty years without learning religion as he ought to know it.

B : Do you suppose that people are ignorant of the things which you mention ?

A : I have no doubt whatever of it. Few people have sufficient knowledge of religion to profit by sermons.

B : Yes, people who are *untaught* and *uncultured* are no doubt ignorant of them.

C : Very well ; is it not the mass of the people whom it is his duty to instruct ?

---

surprised if they show signs of impatience—give us liberty, or give us provender—they are 'hungry sheep' that 'look up and are not fed'; the 'lean and flashy songs' which 'grate' on their pastor's 'pipe' not sufficing."—J. J. BLUNT: *Duties of the Parish Priest*, p. 143.

A : You must add that the greater number of the respectable belong to "the people" in that sense. Three-fourths of an audience are always ignorant of those fundamental truths of religion, which the preacher takes for granted that they know.*

B : Would you wish then that in a large and educated audience a preacher should begin to explain the Catechism?

---

* "My firm belief is that, if you could constrain, I will not say a congregation of rustics, but of the great middle class, or even of the aristocracy, to go through an elementary examination in the most important subjects which can engage the human intellect, the result would be beyond measure startling. I am not speaking lightly when I affirm that few could explain in an intelligent manner why they are Christians, and still fewer why they are Church-people. Of the four Gospels they might manifest some floating and confused knowledge, but most of the books of the Bible would be found to be, for all rational purposes, undiscovered tracts of territory as the wilds of Central Africa. The slightest acquaintance with Church History, Church Biography, Church Literature, or Church Ritual, would be discovered to be exceptional."—TWELLS : *Colloquies,* p. 61.

"Never be afraid of making your explanations of any truth, or fact, or duty, too simple and elementary. One of the most charming popular preachers and speakers that I ever knew, said to me once, that he always took it for granted, that the people knew nothing about the subject on which he was speaking to them. . . . The thoughts of ordinary men on most things not connected with their own profession are very indefinite. Large numbers of persons, who have been accustomed to read the Bible and to listen to preaching all their lives, have the loosest possible acquaintance with the details of biblical history, and their conceptions of doctrinal truth are extremely vague. They are grateful to any man who will make their knowledge of the external facts of Holy Scripture definite, and who will give sharpness and firmness to the outlines of their conceptions of truth."

—DALE: *Lectures* p. 148.

A : I know that there must be a certain adaptation of the matter taught, to the particular occasion; but it is quite possible without offending one's hearers to quote and refer to those historical facts which explain the origin and the institution of all holy things. So far from that enquiry into their origin being unworthy of the notice of an audience, it would give to the greater number of discourses a force and a beauty which are at present wanting to them. We have already made a passing remark to that effect yesterday, especially with regard to the mysteries of the Faith. An audience is neither instructed nor influenced if we do not go back to the beginning in reasoning with them. How, for example, can we make the people understand what the Church says so often after S. Paul that Jesus Christ is our Passover (1 Cor. v. 7), if we do not explain what the Passover of the Jews was, and that it was instituted in order to be a perpetual memorial of the deliverance from Egypt, and to typify a deliverance still more important which was reserved for the Saviour? It is on that account that I said to you that almost everything in religion is of an historical nature. In order then that preachers should thoroughly understand these religious truths, it is absolutely necessary that they should be learned in the Scriptures.

B : Pardon me for interrupting you on this subject of the Holy Scriptures. You told us this morning that they were eloquent. I was delighted to hear you say so, and I should be very glad if you would teach me to recognise their excellences. In what does this eloquence consist? The Latin Bible [*i.e.* the Vulgate] appears to me barbarous in many passages, and I do not discover any refinement at all in the thoughts. What then is it that you admire?

A : The Latin is only a literal version, in which a great many Hebrew and Greek phrases have been retained through reverence for the original. Do you despise Homer because we have him translated into bad French?

B : But the Greek itself (which is the original for the whole of the New Testament) appears to me very bad.

A : I do not dispute it. The Apostles who have written in Greek were like other Greek-speaking Jews of their time, not well acquainted with that language: thence it is that S. Paul says of himself "*Though I be rude in speech yet not in knowledge.*" It is easy to see that S. Paul avows that he had not a complete knowledge of Greek, though he explains in it nevertheless the doctrines which we have in the Holy Scriptures with great exactness to his hearers.

B : But had not the Apostles the Gift of Tongues?

A : No doubt they had it, and it extended even to a great number of private Christians: but as to the tongues which they knew already by natural means, we have ground for believing that God left them to speak these as they had spoken them previously. S. Paul, who was of Tarsus spoke naturally Greek corrupted by the Hellenistic Jews; and we see that he has written in the same dialect. S. Luke appears to have known Greek better.

C: But I have always understood that S. Paul distinctly says in one passage that he put no dependence in eloquence, but relied only upon the simplicity of the Gospel message. Nay, I have heard many people of weight declare that the Holy Scripture is not eloquent at all. *S. Jerome* was punished because he felt a distaste for its simplicity, and preferred Cicero. *S. Augustine* appears in his *Confessions* to have committed the same fault. Has not God chosen to try our faith, not only by the obscurity of the Scriptures, but also by the poorness of their style, as He has done by the poverty of Jesus Christ?

A: Sir, I fear that you are going too far. Whom would you rather believe, S. Jerome punished for having pursued too much in his retreat his taste for the studies of his youth, or S. Jerome consummately skilled in sacred and profane knowledge, who invites Paulinus in an epistle to study the Holy Scriptures, and who promises him more beauties in the Prophets than he had ever found in the poets? Had S. Augustine more weight of authority in his first youth, when the apparent poorness of the style of the Scriptures did, as he says himself, cause him to feel a distaste for them, or when he composed his treatise *On Christian Doctrine?* In that treatise he frequently says* that S. Paul has a marvellous power of persuasion, and that the torrent of his eloquence is capable of making itself felt, even by those who are inattentive. He adds that in S. Paul, wisdom has not sought in the least for beauty of style, but that beauty of style attends and even goes beyond the wisdom. He quotes various grand passages from his Epistles, and makes it evident that in these all the art of heathen orators has been surpassed. He makes two exceptions only in this comparison: the one, that heathen orators have sought purposely for the ornaments of eloquence, while eloquence has followed the utterances of S. Paul and the other sacred writers, naturally and undesignedly: the other, that S. Augustine allows that he did not understand sufficiently well the refinements of the Greek language to be a competent judge whether there be in the Holy Scriptures the rhythm and cadence of those rounded sentences which are to be found in secular writers. I forgot to say that he brings forward this passage of the prophet Amos: "*Woe to them who are at ease in Sion, and trust in the mountains of Samaria!*"† He declares that the

---

* *De Doct. Christ.* B. iv. *et seq.*

† *Ibid.* Amos vi. 1.

Prophet has in this passage surpassed all that is most wonderful in the art of heathen orators.

C: But how do you understand those words of S. Paul: "*Not in the words which man's wisdom teacheth*"? Does he not say to the Corinthians that he is not come to preach Jesus Christ to them with excellency of speech and of wisdom; that he knew nothing among them but Jesus Christ and Him crucified; that his preaching was founded not on the persuasive words of human wisdom, but on the manifest effects of the Spirit and Power of God; so that, he continues, your faith should be founded not at all on the wisdom of man but on the power of God? What is the meaning of these words? How could anyone speak more strongly in altogether disclaiming that art of persuasion which you are here declaring to be necessary? I confess that I was edified when you condemned all those affected ornaments with which vanity seeks to adorn discourses: but that which follows does not maintain so pious a beginning. You are going to make of preaching an art wholly human, and the Apostolic simplicity will be excluded from it.

A: You take it ill that I should set a great value upon eloquence, and for my part I am greatly edified by the zeal with which you blame me on that account. Nevertheless it will not be amiss to give mutual explanations upon that point. I see many excellent people, who, like you, suppose that eloquent preachers injure the simplicity of the

Gospel. When each of us understands what the other means, we shall soon be in agreement. What do you understand by simplicity? and what do you understand by eloquence?

C: By simplicity I understand a discourse without art and without splendour. By eloquence, on the contrary, I understand a discourse full of art and of ornaments.

A: When you ask for a simple discourse do you wish for one without order, without connection, without solid and conclusive proofs, without a suitable method of instructing the ignorant? Do you wish for a preacher who has no pathos whatever, and who does not even attempt to touch the hearts of his hearers?

C: Quite the contrary; I ask for a discourse which shall be both touching and instructive.

A: You wish then that it should be eloquent: for we have already agreed that eloquence is only the art of instructing and persuading men while touching their hearts.

C: I agree that it is necessary both to touch and to instruct; but I should wish that this should be done by an Apostolic simplicity and without art.

A: Let us see then whether art and Apostolic simplicity are incompetible. What do you understand by "art"?

C: I understand certain rules which the human mind has discovered, and which it follows in a discourse in order to render it more beautiful and polished.

A : If you understand by art only those expedients which render a discourse more polished and agreeable to the hearers* I do not contest what you say, and I agree that art ought to be banished from sermons since that vanity, as we have agreed, is unworthy of eloquence and therefore much more unworthy of the Apostolic ministry. It was expressly upon that subject in fact that I had so long an argument with *B.* But if you understand by "art" and "eloquence" what all the skilful among the ancients have understood by them, it will be proper to bring other considerations into view.

C : What then did they understand by them?

A : According to them, the art of eloquence consists in those means which have been discovered by reflection and experience in order to render a discourse suitable to persuade men of the truth,

---

* This rule, however, is diametrically opposed to a great mass of modern opinion. Thus a character introduced in a work already quoted, as a representative of keen men of the world, is made to say: "My notion is that sermons should always be on topics of the day. We are not living in the time of the patriarchs, nor yet of the prophets; no, nor even of the early Christians. We are living in this reckless, rushing, helter-skelter nineteenth century, and our parsons should select their subjects accordingly. If they caught up the events of the past week, and gave them a sort of moral or religious turn, they would scarcely have the listless audiences that confront them now."

—TWELLS : *Colloquies,* p. 46.

and to arouse the love of it in their hearts; and these are the very same objects that you wish to find pursued by a preacher. Did you not say to me at that very time that there were needful in a discourse both an orderly method of instruction, solid reasoning and pathetic appeals, that is to say, those means which touch and influence hearts? Now eloquence consists of nothing else than these. Recall that to your memory if you please.

C: I see clearly now to what elements you reduce eloquence. Under that grave and serious form I think it worthy of the pulpit and even necessary if instruction is to have a good result. But how do you understand that passage from S. Paul against eloquence? I have already quoted the words; is it not explicit?

A: Permit me to begin by asking you a question.

C: Willingly.

A: Is it not the fact that S. Paul reasons admirably in his Epistles? Are not the arguments masterly which he carries on against the heathen philosophers, and against the Jews in the Epistle to the Romans? And his observations on the inability of the Mosaic Law to justify men, are they not full of power?

C: No doubt they are.

A: And again, what he says in the Epistle to the Hebrews, on the insufficiency of the ancient sacrifices, on the repose promised by David to the people of God, surpassing that which they enjoyed in Palestine from the time of Joshua, on the priesthood of Aaron and that of Melchisedek, and on the spiritual and eternal covenant which was necessarily to succeed to that carnal covenant which Moses had instituted for a time ; are not all these instances of acute and profound reasoning ?

C : Unquestionably they are.

A : S. Paul then had no wish to exclude wisdom and the power of reasoning from the preaching of the Gospel.

C : That is apparent from his own example.

A : What then was your reason for supposing that he would have eloquence excluded from preaching, rather than wisdom ?

C : It was that he rejects eloquence in the passage which I asked you to explain.

A : But does he not reject wisdom also ? No doubt he does ; the passage is still more decisive against wisdom and human reasoning than against eloquence. Yet he did not cease for himself both to reason and to be eloquent. You agree to the one assertion, and S. Augustine assures you of the other.

C : You enable me to see the difficulty very clearly, but you do not give me any light upon it. How do you explain it ?

A : Thus : S. Paul reasoned, S. Paul persuaded; thus he was essentially an excellent philosopher and orator. But his preaching, as he states in the passage now in question, was founded neither on human reasoning nor on human persuasion ; it was a ministry, of which the whole force came from on high. The conversion of the whole world was to be, according to the prophecies, the great miracle of Christianity. It was the kingdom of God, which came down from heaven, and was to bring into subjection to the true God all the nations of the earth. Jesus Christ crucified, when preached to the nations, was to draw all men unto Him; but how? Simply by the unique virtue of His Cross. The philosophers had reasoned, without converting men and without being converted themselves; the Jews had been the depositaries of a law which did, indeed, make manifest their sins, but without bringing the remedy : such was the state of the earth; it was convicted of error and of corruption. Jesus Christ came with His Cross: that is to say, He came poor, humble, and suffering; and this, on our account, to put to silence our vain and presumptuous reason. He did not at all reason like the philosophers; but by His miracles, and by His grace, He taught as one having authority. He showed that He was above all. In order to confound the shallow wisdom of men, He opposed to it the folly and the disgrace of the Cross, that is to say, the example of His profound humiliations. That which the world regarded as folly, and which scandalized it the most, was to be the very means of bringing it back to God. Man needs to be cured of his pride, and of his love for the things of this present world. By this means God takes hold of his heart and mind; He shows to him His Son crucified. His Apostles walk in His footsteps, and preach Him. They avail themselves of no human resources: neither philosophy, nor eloquence, nor political advantages, nor riches, nor authority. God was jealous of His work, and would have it owe its success to Himself only: He chose that which was weak as the means, and rejected that which was strong, so as to manifest more plainly His own power. He summons that which is not, to convert the world, as He did to bring it into being. Thus the work [of salvation] necessarily has this Divine character, that it is founded upon nothing which is valuable according to the flesh. To have supported the preaching of the Gospel on the resources of nature would have been, according to S. Paul, to weaken and lose the miraculous power of the Cross. It was needful that the Gospel should of itself make its way into hearts, without any human preparation, and by this prodigy should teach the world that it came from God. Thus human wisdom was confounded and reproved. What inference ought we to draw from this? That the conversion of the nations and the establishment of the Church were due in no respect to the argument and persuasive powers of men. It is not that the greater number of those who preached Jesus Christ were not endowed with a measure of wisdom and of eloquence: but that they did not put their confidence in that wisdom and that eloquence; nor seek at all to give efficacy to their words by means of these. Everything was made to rest, as S. Paul says, not on the persuasive eloquence of human philosophy, but on the influence of the Spirit and power of God; that is to say, upon miracles which were visible to the eye, and to the inward working of grace.

C: To rely then, upon human wisdom and eloquence in preaching is, according to your view, to lose the power of the cross of Christ.

A: I think so, without doubt; the ministry of the Word is founded wholly upon Faith. The essential preparation of the preacher is in prayer, in the purification of his own heart, in the expecting of every good result from Heaven, in arming himself with the sword of the Word of God, not with any weapon of his own. But although the inward results of the Gospel are to be looked for only from pure grace, and the efficacy of the Word of God, yet there are certain things which man, on his side, ought to do.

C: So far you have spoken well; but I see clearly that you are now going back into your former views.

A: I am not aware that I have left them at all.

Do you not believe that the work of your salvation depends upon grace?

C : Yes, that is a part of our Faith.

A : Nevertheless you recognise that it is the part of prudence to choose certain right paths in life and to avoid occasions of evil? Do you not think that we ought to watch and pray? But when we shall have watched and prayed, shall we have rendered the mystery of grace needless? Without doubt we shall not. We owe all to God, but God subjects us to an outward order of human means. The Apostles did not seek at all for the empty pomp and frivolous graces of heathen orators; they did not addict themselves to the subtle reasonings of the philosophers, who made everything depend upon those arguments in which they refined everything away, as S. Paul says: they were content to preach Jesus Christ,* but they did so with all that power and magnificence which we see in the

---

* "Our method of preaching is not that by which Christianity was propagated; yet the genius of Christianity is not changed. There was nothing in the primitive method set or formal. The primitive bishop stood up and read the Gospel, or some other portion of Scripture, and pressed on the hearers, with great earnestness and affection, a few plain and forcible truths evidently resulting from that portion of the Divine Word; we take a text and make an oration. Edification was then the object of both speaker and hearers; and while this continues to be the object, no better method can be found. A parable or history, or passage of Scripture, thus illustrated and enforced, is the best method of introducing truth to any people who are ignorant of it, and of setting it home with power on those who know it, and not formal, doctrinal, argumentative discourses. Truth and sympathy are the soul of an

language of Scripture. It is true that they had no need of a preparation for the exercise of that ministry, because the Holy Spirit, who descended visibly upon them, gave them " in the same hour, the words which they ought to speak." The difference then between the Apostles and their successors in the ministry is that those successors, not being miraculously inspired as they were, have need to prepare themselves and to fill their minds with the doctrine and the spirit of the Scriptures in order to construct their discourses.* But this

---

efficacious ministry. . . . A primitive bishop would have been shocked with one of our sermons; and such is our taste, we should be shocked with his. They brought forward Scripture, we bring forward our statements. They directed all their observations to throw light on Scripture, we quote Scripture to throw light on our observations. More faith and more grace would make us better preachers, for ' out of the abundance of the heart the mouth speaketh.' Chrysostom's was the right method. Leighton's ' Lectures on Peter ' approach very near to this method."—REV. RICHARD CECIL: *Remains*, p. 180.

* " It sometimes happens that particular doctrines are unpopular at particular periods, or in particular places. There is scarcely any great truth that has not occasionally suffered in this way. The depravity of human nature. justification by faith, the claims of an outward and visible Church of Christ, the resurrection of the body, the efficacy of holy baptism, the laying on of hands both at confirmation and ordination, the preciousness of the blessed Eucharist, all these and others have in turn been under a cloud, and may be again: but whatever articles of faith the preacher believes to *be* articles of faith, not mere human traditions or private idiosyncrasies, these he must teach to his congregation, as opportunity offers, whether they will bear, or whether they will forbear."—TWELLS: *Colloquies*, p. 141.

"To evade dogma, then, or to hold it of little account, is a defect in the preacher, who is never, or hardly ever, successful, except he be

preparation ought never to lead them to speak less simply than the Apostles. Would not you be content, provided that preachers were never more full of ornaments in their discourses than were S. Peter, S. Paul, S. James, S. Jude, and S. John?

C: I quite agree that I ought to be content with that; and I confess that as eloquence consists only, as you say, in the order and vigour of the words by which the speaker endeavours to persuade and to touch his hearers, it ought no longer to scandalize me as it used to do. I have always thought that eloquence was an art altogether secular.

A: There are two classes of people who have that idea. The first are pretenders to oratory; and we have already seen how greatly they are mistaken in seeking for eloquence by the use of a meaningless parade of words. The second are those well-meaning people who are insufficiently acquainted with the

---

dogmatic. The moral essayist in the pulpit is common enough now-a-days; he is often a literary artist, and attracts many people by his grace of diction and richness of ideas. He never shocks or frightens them, for his real gospel is that of modern culture. So it was with Menander and the genteel comedy of the Greeks, when the stage had given up all idea of reforming mankind, and confined itself to pictures of human life. There are great lessons to be gained by such portraiture, and by the graceful but forcible exposure of the weakness and folly of men. But this is not preaching, and will not preserve for the preacher the great vantage ground he once possessed as the leader of earnest men."
—MAHAFFY, J. P.: *An Essay on the Decay of Modern Preaching*, p. 118.

subject; and with regard to them you see that while they, influenced by humility, renounce eloquence as being an useless pomp of words, they virtually seek for true eloquence, since they desire to touch and to influence their hearers.

C : Now I fully understand all that you wish to insist upon. But let us return to the eloquence of the Scriptures.

A : Nothing is more useful in helping us to appreciate this than to have a taste for the antique simplicity: especially the reading of the ancient Greek writers is of great service in attaining this. I say the *ancient* Greek writers, because those Greeks whom the Romans so despised, with good reason, and whom they called *Græculi*, were wholly degenerate. As I said to you before, it is needful to know Homer, Plato, Xenophon and the other writers of earlier times; after that the Scripture will no longer cause you any surprise. In these two classes of writings the customs, the modes of narration, the vivid pictures of great subjects, the vigorous appeals, are almost or entirely the same. The difference existing between them is wholly to the advantage of the Scriptures; these infinitely surpass all the others in simplicity, in vivacity, in grandeur. Even Homer has never approached the sublimity of Moses in his Canticles, particularly the last (Deut. xxxii. 1-13), which all the children of the Israelites were obliged to learn by heart. No

Greek or Latin ode has ever been able to attain the loftiness of thought and language which is found in the Psalms. For example, that one which commences thus : *The Lord even the most High God hath spoken and called the world from the rising of the sun unto the going down thereof* (Ps. L.), surpasses every purely human utterance. Neither Homer nor any other poet has ever equalled Isaiah when he paints the majesty of God, to whose eyes kingdoms are only as a grain of dust, and the entire universe as a tabernacle, which to-day is pitched, and to-morrow carried away (Isa. xl. 9). Sometimes that Prophet has all the beauty and tenderness of an eclogue, in his smiling pictures of peace ; and anon he rises to an elevation where all such things are far beneath his feet. What is there in the secular literature of the ancient world, that is at all comparable to the sensitive Jeremiah deploring the woes of his people (Lam. i. 1), or to Nahum beholding from afar in his prophetic vision the walls of stately Nineveh falling under the efforts of a countless army (Nah. ii. 3) ? We seem even to behold that army ; to hear the clang of armour and of chariots ; the picture is so vivid that it fires the imagination ; it leaves Homer far behind. Again, read the account of Daniel pronouncing to Belshazzar that the vengeance of God was about to fall upon him (Dan. v. 17), and then seek, in the sublimest works of antiquity, anything worthy to be compared with it. And further, all is consistent in the Scripture ; everything has the character that properly belongs to it; the history, the details of the legislation, the descriptions, the passionate passages, the mysteries, the discourses on morality. In a word, there is as much difference between the Prophets and the secular poets as between true enthusiasm and false. The former are veritably inspired, and give expression with power to some truth divinely revealed: the latter raise themselves by an effort above their ordinary standard, and thus make their human weakness the more conspicuous. Only the Second Book of the Maccabees—the Book of Wisdom, especially towards the end—and the beginning of that of Ecclesiasticus, have any traces of that inflation of style which the Greeks, then already dethroned, had spread throughout the East, where their language had established itself during the period of their predominance. I should have been pleased to say more to you of these matters: but they must be read in order to be fully appreciated.

B: I am impatient to look into them for myself. No doubt this study ought to be more attentively pursued than is done.

C: I can well imagine that the Old Testament is written with that magnificence, and contains those vivid pictures of life, of which you speak. But you say nothing of the simplicity which marks the words of Jesus Christ.

A : That simplicity of style is wholly in the antique manner: it is conformed to that of Moses and the Prophets, whose very expressions Jesus Christ often adopts: but although simple and familiar, it is sublime and very figurative in many passages. It would be easy to show in detail, if we had the books before us, that there is no preacher of our age who, in his most elaborately prepared discourses, has been as figurative as was Jesus Christ in His popular preaching. I do not speak at all of the discourses reported by S. John, in which almost all is manifestly Divine. I speak of the more familiar discourses recorded by the other Evangelists. The Apostles have written in the same manner, with this difference: Jesus Christ being master of His teaching, imparts it calmly and with composure. He says what seems good to Him, and He says it without effort; He speaks of the kingdom of heaven and its glory as of the house of His Father. All those marks of greatness which astonish us are natural to Him: He is born to them, and as He Himself assures us, speaks that which He has seen and knows. The Apostles, on the contrary, seem to bend under the weight of the truths which have been revealed to them: they want words, and cannot fully express the conceptions they have in their minds. From this cause come inversions of phrase, indistinct expressions, loose ends of discourse which they are unable to round off. All this irregularity of style, in the case of S. Paul and the other Apostles, marks the fact that their minds are drawn onwards by the Spirit of God; and notwithstanding these small irregularities of style, all that they say is noble, energetic, and touching. In the Apocalypse are found the same magnificence and enthusiasm as in the prophets: the expressions used are often the same, and not seldom the relation between them assists the understanding of each. So you see that eloquence belongs not exclusively to the books of the Old Testament, but is found also in the New.

C: Granted that the Scriptures are eloquent, what conclusion would you draw from that?

A: That those who have to preach ought, without hesitation, to imitate or rather to borrow their eloquence.

C: And also, I suppose, to pick out for quotation the passages which are the most beautiful.

A: The Scriptures are disfigured by not allowing Christians to become acquainted with them except in detached passages. These passages, although they are so beautiful, cannot make the whole of their beauty felt, because they stand alone, and the context of them is not presented to the people as well. For all is consecutive in the Scripture, and that close connection between its parts is the grandest and most marvellous quality of all. For want of knowing this, passages are taken in a sense quite opposite to their own: they are made to say everything that the preacher chooses; and he is contented with certain ingenious glosses which, being arbitrary, have no power to persuade men, and to reform character.*

B: Then what would you have preachers do? Should they only follow literally the text of Scripture?

A: Wait a little. I should desire at least that they should not content themselves with weaving together passages agreeing with each other; that they should explain the principles and the mutual connections of the doctrines of Scripture; that they should adopt the spirit, the style, and the illustrations of it; and that all their discourses should be helpful in giving a knowledge of and a taste for it. A preacher could not fail then to be eloquent; for that would be to imitate the perfect model of eloquence.

B: But for that purpose it would be needful, as I said to you, to explain the texts of Scripture consecutively to the people.

A: I should not wish that all preachers should take up that task. It is possible to preach sermons on the Scripture without explaining the whole of Scripture, one book after another. But it must be confessed that it would be quite another thing if Pastors, following the ancient usage, were in the

---

* See Notes 1 and 2.

habit of commenting on the whole of Scripture in order to the people. Imagine to yourself what great authority a man would have, who was in the habit of saying nothing of his own devising; but who set himself simply to follow and to explain the thoughts and the words of God Himself. Besides this, he would accomplish two objects at once: in explaining the truths of Scripture he would also explain the text; and would accustom Christians always to join together the text and the meaning. What an advantage to them to become accustomed to nourish their souls with that sacred bread! An audience which should have already learned to understand how to explain all the principal institutions of the ancient Law, would be in a very different state of preparation to profit by the explanation of the New, than the greater number of Christians at the present day. The preacher of whom we spake a little while ago had this defect among his great qualities, that his sermons are fine arguments about religion, but are not all composed of religion itself. They are devoted to sketches of morality, and too little occupied in explaining the dogmatic principles of Evangelical doctrine.

B: The reason of that is that it is much more easy to depict the disorders of the world than to explain with precision the depths of Christian doctrine. For the one, all that is needful is experience of wordly business, and words to describe it : for the other, is required a serious and profound mediation upon the Holy Scriptures. Few people know religion, as a whole, sufficiently to explain it well. Such a person (as the former) writes sermons which are beautiful, but would not know how to draw up a solid and orthodox catechism, much less a homily.

A: You have stated the case exactly. The greater number of sermons are philosophical arguments. In many cases the Scripture is never quoted, except when the conclusion has been reached, and that merely for courtesy or for ornament. Then it is no longer the Word of God that is preached: it is the word and the devices of men.*

C: You will grant, I hope, that those people labour only to supersede the Cross of Christ.

A: I agree to all you say of them. I restrict myself to the eloquence of the Scriptures, which preachers of the Gospel ought to imitate. Thus we are agreed; provided that you do not excuse certain jealous preachers, who, under the pretext of observing Apostolic simplicity, neglect to study solidly either the doctrine of the Scriptures, or the wonderful manner of influencing the hearts of men, of which God has given us there the pattern. They imagine that they have only to shout at the top of their voices, and to talk of the devil and of hell often

---

* "Some one said that Gibbon's style was a style in which it was impossible to speak the truth."—DALE: *Lectures*, p. 177.

enough, in order to convert souls; but it is in the Scripture that we should learn how to make those strong and grave impressions. There also we may learn admirably how to make our instructions vivid and popular, without causing them to lose the dignity and power which they ought to have.* For

---

* "To this feeling, the *Excessive Love of Variety*, may be ascribed the vulgar habit of introducing anecdotes in the pulpit—anecdotes which are not only foolish and beside the point, but often practically untrue, inasmuch as the preacher always explains the facts, and the explanation may be palpably invented. Anecdotage in the pulpit gratifies only the most ignorant and vulgar of hearers, and from vulgar I mean to exclude all those of however low degree who come to hear seriously for the sake of spiritual benefit. . . . . . . Of a similar character are those excursions into politics, into popular science, into secular poetry, which sometimes occupy whole discourses, and which are listened to with attention and amusement, but seldom with profit. If these things be used in illustration of great truths, they are evidences of large culture in the preacher, and also have their real value. But to make variety the main object of preaching is to forget that eternal truths require more than a passing notice. The broad lines upon which human conduct should be built must be often and often explained and enforced."—MAHAFFY, p. 125.

> "For wisdom dealt with mortal powers,
> Where truth in closest words shall fail,
> When *truth embodied in a tale*
> Shall enter in at lowly doors."—*In Memoriam*.

"Nor is it merely at 'lowly doors' that 'truth embodied in a tale' finds easier entrance than truth, which appears in the form of abstract propositions. God, who knows as we cannot know the mystery of our nature, has revealed Himself to mankind in a supernatural history. The Revelation which we have to illustrate, and which furnishes the very substance of all our preaching, is not a series of theological dogmas or ethical principles; it is in the main a record of how God has dealt with individual men, with nations, and with the human race.

want of knowing this, they often only bewilder their hearers: leave no distinct impressions of truth in their minds, but only of fear, which soon pass away. That simplicity which they affect is then nothing but an ignorance and rudeness which is, in fact, a form of tempting God. Nothing can excuse those people, except the goodness of their intentions.* Before preaching it is needful to have studied and meditated upon the Holy Scriptures long and deeply. A priest who has a full and accurate knowledge of them,† and who has the

---

Above all, it is the story of the earthly life, the death, the Resurrection, and the Ascension into Heaven of Our Lord Jesus Christ—God manifest in the flesh."—R. W. DALE: *Lectures on Preaching*, p. 50.

* "Read such books as will assist you to a complete mastery of the language in which you preach. No man has a right to set himself up as a public teacher, or to allow others to do it, without being master of some vehicle of expression; or, at least striving earnestly for the mastery. The free school, the public library, an educated pulpit, the masterpieces of the ages reduced to a minimum of cost, have rendered life-long sins against grammar and rhetoric inexcusable. The preacher cannot afford to have his language blue-pencilled by nursery fledgelings. The barber who drops his razor, the artist who steps on his pallet and stumbles over his easel, and the sculptor who is reckless with his chisels are fit companions for the preacher who is a tyro in pulpit letters."

—REV. J. M. DRIVER.

† By way of contrast, take the following contemporary view of preaching. It is manifest how far the sentiment differs from that in the text: "In our day preaching must be full of humanity. That is to say, the truths presented must stand in vital relation to the life we are living. There have been periods when men had their being in the realm of the abstract and the controversial; when they were interested in doctrine for the sake of the doctrines. For better or worse, the

ability to speak, joined with the authority of his ministry and of his good example, will have no need of long preparation in order to preach excellent sermons: it is easy to speak fluently upon subjects which one knows well and feels deeply upon. A subject like that of religion is especially rich in lofty thoughts, and prompt to arouse noble sentiments; and it is these which constitute true eloquence. In a preacher should be found a father who speaks to his children with tenderness, and not merely a declaimer who uses emphasis only as an instrument of rhetoric. Therefore it is much to be wished that there should be no pastors who do not constantly feed their flocks according to the need of each. All that would be needed for that purpose would be to choose for Pastors only priests who have the gift of utterance. Where this is not the case, two evils follow : the one that there are Pastors who preach with little ability or who do not preach at all; and these are little esteemed : the other that the function of preacher when voluntarily assumed draws into it I know not how many vain and ambitious minds. You know that the ministry of the Word was for many ages reserved to Bishops, especially in the West. You remember the example

---

world has moved on, and if it listens patiently to the exposition of biblical doctrine, it is for the sake of its practical bearings. The surest way, therefore, for any man to discredit his ministry, is to manifest a tendency to special pleading, to revel in the domain of the abstract."—E. G. SELDEN.

of *S. Augustine*, who, contrary to the common rule, was induced to preach while he was only a priest, because his predecessor Valerius was a foreigner who did not preach fluently: this was the commencement of that custom in the West. In the East priests were authorised to preach much sooner. The sermons which *S. Chrysostom* delivered at Antioch, although only as yet a priest, are a sign of this.

C: I am like you of that opinion. It would be desirable that only Pastors should, as a rule, be allowed to preach; that would be the means of restoring to the pulpit the simplicity and authority which it ought to have: because Pastors who added to their experience of duty, and of the guidance of souls, the knowledge of the Scriptures, would speak in a manner much more suitable to the needs of their hearers; instead of which, preachers who have only theory to go upon, do not suit themselves at all to the minds of their hearers, enter very little into their difficulties, and speak in a more vague and general manner. Not to mention the special weight attached to the voice of a Pastor, these are strong reasons for preferring their sermons to those of others. What is the advantage of having so many young preachers without experience, without knowledge, without sanctity? It would be much better to have fewer sermons and to have them better.

B: But there are many preachers who are not

Pastors, and who preach with excellent results. How many Religious even there are who occupy pulpits must worthily!

C: Yes, that is very true, but I would make them Pastors. Those are the very people whom it would be desirable to put, even against their will, into posts where they would have the charge of souls. Were there not in former times sought for among the solitaries, those men who were fit to be set in the Sees of the Church?

A: It does not belong to us to adjust matters of discipline: each period has its customs adapted to its own needs. Let us respect for our part all the tolerances of the Church; and without indulging a spirit of criticism let us go on to complete our view of a true preacher.

C: It seems to me, as far as the subjects which you have already mentioned are concerned, it is already complete.

A: Let us hear then, what is your idea of it.

C: I should desire that a man should have devoted himself, during his youth, to the serious study of all that might be of service to him in the Greek and Latin poetry and eloquence.

A: That is not necessary. It is true that when those studies are seriously pursued, they are of great advantage even for the understanding of the Scriptures, as S. Basil has shown in a treatise which he has written expressly on that subject.* But after all it may be passed over; and in the earlier ages of the Church they were in fact altogether omitted. Those who had studied these subjects when they were in the world have drawn from them great advantages for religion when they afterwards became Pastors. But it was not permitted to those who were ignorant of them to acquire them when they were already engaged in the study of sacred literature.† There was a persuasion that the Scripture was sufficient; and on that account it is that you see in the "Apostolical Constitutions" an exhortation to the faithful not to read heathen authors at all. The book we have already quoted (B. i. c. 6) says: "If you wish for history, for legislation, for moral precepts, for eloquence, for poetry, you will find them all in the Scriptures." In fact, there is no need, as we have already seen, to seek elsewhere for help in forming the taste and the judgment, even for the attainment of eloquence. S. Augustine (B. iv. n. 8) says that the smaller is a man's own store of knowledge the more he ought to enrich it from the sacred oracles; and that, being himself so humble a person to expound such great subjects, he needs to grow fitter by this authority of Scripture. But excuse me for having interrupted you, and please to continue.

---

* *On the Reading of the Works of Heathen Writers.*—Hom. 24.
† S. Augustine *de Doct. Christ.* B. ii. n. 58.

C: Well, let us suppose that we content ourselves with the study of Scripture; but will you not add that of the Fathers?

A : Doubtless, they are the channels *(canaux)* of tradition; it is through their writings we learn the manner in which the Church has interpreted the Scriptures in all ages.

C: But is a person necessarily obliged always to expound every passage according to the interpretations which they have given of it? It seems to me that frequently one of them gives a spiritual sense, and another a sense entirely different. Which is to be chosen? For if they are all to be stated he will never have done.

A : When it is said that the Scripture must always be expounded in conformity to the doctrine of the Fathers, what is referred to is *their constant and uniform doctrine*. They often give "pious meanings" which are not literal, nor founded on the doctrine of prophetical forecasts, or the mysteries of the Faith. They are, in fact, arbitrary; and therefore there is no obligation to follow them, since in these points they do not follow each other. But in those passages in which they express the sentiment of the Church on some doctrine of the Faith, or on the principles of conduct, it is not permissible to explain the Scripture in a sense contrary to their doctrine. That is how their authority is to be recognized.

C: That seems to me very clear. I should wish that a priest, before he comes to preach, should be thoroughly acquainted with their doctrine, in order to conform himself to it; and farther, that he should even study their principles of conduct, their rules of discipline, and their method of instruction.

A: Undoubtedly: they are our masters. They were men of lofty minds, great souls full of heroic sentiments, persons who had a marvellous experience of the minds and characters of men, who had acquired great authority, and great power of utterance. It is even evident that they had considerable culture; that is to say, they were perfectly instructed in all the proprieties, whether of correspondence or of public speaking, of private life, or of the performance of civil functions. Doubtless, all that training must have rendered them extremely eloquent, and very well fitted to persuade others. And their writings display a degree of politeness, not only of words, but of character and sentiments, which is not found at all in writers of the following ages. That politeness, which agrees perfectly with plainness and simplicity of disposition, and which rendered them acceptable and winning, had important consequences for the good of religion. That is a quality in them which cannot be too much studied. In them, after the Scriptures, will be found the pure sources of good sermons.

C: When a man shall have acquired that

foundation of knowledge, and shall have edified the Church by an example of virtues, he will be in a condition to expound the Gospel with much authority and with good results. He will also have been suitably exercised (it is very important to add) by the delivery of familiar instructions and Conferences, and will thus have gained a certain facility and freedom of utterance, sufficient to enable him to speak effectively. Again, I understand that such persons, being occupied in every detail of the ministry, in the administration of Sacraments, the guidance of souls, the visiting of the sick and dying, really have not time carefully to prepare sermons and commit them to memory. It is out of the abundance of the heart, in their case, that the mouth ought to speak; that is, it should impart unto the people that knowledge of the Gospel which the preacher possesses, and make them conscious of that affectionate solicitude for his hearers, which his heart feels.* On the question, which you touched

---

* "The fruit of the Spirit is not negative, but positive. It is zeal in love; it is humility; it is mind-influence; it is disinterestedness; it is activity in doing good. As you rise from the animal towards the higher forms of men, the natures that are developed must be positive, not negative. A man may have a garden with not a single bit of purslane in it from one end to the other; with not a single Canada thistle in it; with not a pig-weed in it. A man may have a garden without one bad thing in it—and without a good thing in it either, not a flower nor a fruit. Now, to get your weeds out of the way is all right; but the weeds are to be got out in order that the ground may be occupied by positive blossoms and fruit. Not doing wrong is right; but it is a lower right. It is simply keeping under the weeds, as it were, of a man's

upon yesterday, of learning sermons by heart, I have had the curiosity to look out a passage of *S. Augustine*, which I had formerly read : and this is the sense of it. He lays down that preachers

---

disposition, while the real thing which a man should seek to do should be to produce positive virtues. But veneration does not produce these; and therefore it is not, when the soul moves in complex ways, fitted to be the master. It cannot drive the soul when its different faculties are all abroad, and are variously engaged. It takes another charioteer. So neither can you centre the character round about ideality—the artist feeling—the taste feeling—the sense of beauty and propriety. At certain stages of civilisation men naturally make that pre-eminent, and, as I have said, it may become a powerful auxiliary to the spiritual emotions, to a much larger extent than it is; but as a master-centre, as a sovereign in the soul, it is feeble. As a restrainer, as a harmoniser, as a guide and governor, it is a power indeed. And that which is true of beauty is just as true of conscience. Gentlemen, we hear a great deal said about conscience; we hear a great deal said about the lack of conscience; and I believe that the foundations of character ought to be laid on conscience, just as the parlour and nursery ought to be laid on oak sills; but I should as soon think of bringing up my children on planks and timbers in the parlour and nursery, laying their bare limbs down on these hard timbers and planks, as to attempt to make a rich, sweet, lovely, and lustrous character simply on conscience, which is, in its essential nature, cold, hard, condemnatory, and which comes into alliance with the malign passions much more naturally than with the benign elements. Its chemical affinities are with the bottom, and not often with the top. At any rate they have by practice and habit been made to ally themselves very much with the lower qualities of the mind. The soul will not own conscience as its master. Neither will fear or superstition do to be made the centre about which to harmonise all the faculties of a man's soul. There is but one real centre—Love."

—BEECHER : *Lectures*, p. 215.

"A sermon that has more head infused into it than heart will not come home with efficacy to the hearers. 'You must do so and so;

ought to speak more clearly and forcibly than other people; because as custom and respect do not permit them to be questioned, they ought to be constantly on their guard against not sufficiently adapting themselves to the needs of their hearers.* "That is why," he says, "those who learn their sermons word for word, so that they are unable to repeat and still further explain a particular truth until they can see that it is understood, deprive themselves of a great advantage." That clearly shows you that S. Augustine thought it sufficient

---

such and such advantages will result from doing it.' This is cold, dead, and spiritless, when it stands alone, or even when it is most prominent. Let the preacher's head be stored with wisdom; but above all, let his heart so feel his subject, that he may infuse life and interest into it, by speaking like one who actually possesses and feels what he says."

—CECIL: *Remains*, p. 209.

* "Preaching, to-day, must be crisp in style and compact in thought. No man of our generation can write in his diary of having 'sweetly discoursed for two hours' in the pulpit. If one should begin such a sermon with a full house, he would find it ingloriously vacated before reaching his 'conclusion.' The stately and elaborate methods of introduction and development indulged in by our ancestors in the ministry would be accounted insufferably tedious, and the verbose 'improvement,' once so effective, would dissipate any wholesome impressions previously created. There must be no appearance of underestimating the value of time; it must be redeemed by an eager pressing on toward the goal sighted from the starting-point of the text. The movement of the preacher must be swift enough at least to keep him always in advance of his quick-witted hearers. If he has anything to say he must *say* it. Any dawdling with platitudes and commonplaces, any indolent prolixity, any cheap padding of the discourse, will not be tolerated— even by a long-suffering people. The age is too busy for a leisurely dealing even with divine things."—E. G. SELDEN.

to prepare the matter of his subject in his mind, without burdening his memory with all the words of his sermons. Even although the rules of true eloquence should require something more than this, those of the ministry of the Gospel would not permit us to go farther. As for me, I have long been of your opinion upon this matter. While Christianity has so many pressing wants : while the priest, who ought to be a man of God prepared for every good work, ought to be hastening to root up ignorant scandals from the field of the Church; I regard it as being altogether unworthy of him to pass his life in his study, engaged in rounding his periods, in retouching his descriptions, in settling his divisions. For from the time that he joins the ranks of that class of preacher he will have time for no other employment, for no other labours or study: his occupation and his pleasure it frequently is to deliver repeatedly the same sermons. When the hearer knows beforehand every phrase and every appeal of a discourse, what room is there for eloquence? How can there be any possibility of surprising, of awing, of softening, of taking hold of, and finally, of persuading men? That is, indeed, a strange way of concealing art and allowing nature to speak. For my part, I say frankly, I am scandalized by all this. What! shall the steward of the mysteries of God sink into a slothful declaimer, jealous of his reputation, desirous of a vain pomp of words? Shall he not venture to speak to his people of their God, without having all his words set ready for him in order, and his lesson learned by heart like a boy at school?

A : Your zeal delights me : and what you say is very true. We must not, however, speak too strongly: there must be consideration shown for many persons of merit and even of piety, who, deferring to custom, are led by example to practise in good faith the method which you rightly blame. But I am ashamed to interrupt you so often. Pray continue.

C : I would have a preacher expound the entire circle of religious truths, state them in a plain and striking manner, point out the original institution of doctrines and practices, the succession of facts, and the handing on of tradition, so that in thus declaring the origin and ground of religion, he may destroy the objections of unbelievers without openly attempting to attack them, and thus, perhaps, scandalizing the uncultured among the faithful.

A : You are quite right; because the proper way to prove the truth of religion is to state it clearly. It manifests its own truth when the idea of it is rightly given. All other proofs, not being drawn from the nature and the circumstances of religion itself, are foreign to it. For example, the best proof of the Creation of the world, the Deluge, and the miracles of Moses, is the nature of those miracles, and the simple and impartial manner in which the history of them is written. A man who is wise and unprejudiced need only read them in order to feel that they are true.

C. I should wish, also, that a preacher should explain industriously and in order to the people every detail of the Gospel and the mysteries of the Faith; the origin and the institution of the Sacraments; the traditions, the discipline, the service and the ceremonies of the Church. Thus the faithful will be forearmed against objections. This will put them in a condition to render a reason for their belief, and will even produce an effect upon those among heretics who are not obstinate. All these instructions will strengthen faith, will give a high idea of religion, and enable the people to profit and gain edification by all that they see in the Church. Instead of this, with the superficial instruction which is given to them, they comprehend scarcely anything at all of what they see, and have only a very confused idea of what a preacher means by what he says to them. The giving of these courses of instruction is the principal reason why I would have preaching left to persons settled in each parish, such as Pastors. I have often remarked that there is no art or science in the world which is not taught by its professors in regular order, according to a fixed method and upon settled principles: it is only religion which is not thus taught to the faithful. A little dry catechism is given to them in childhood, which they learn by heart without understanding the meaning of it; and after that they have no farther instruction whatever, except vague and unconnected sermons. I should wish, as you have said so often, that the first elements of their religion should be taught to Christians, and that they should thus be led in due order up to the highest mysteries.

A : That is exactly what was done in earlier ages. The commencement was made by catechizing, after which Pastors were accustomed to teach the Gospel in regular order* by means of Homilies.

---

* "You should make a practice of reading the Bible frequently through—the several books of which it is composed successively in their order—a practice which I am convinced you will find advantageous in various ways. A volume of knowledge, an intimacy with your whole subject, will thus gradually accumulate upon you, which will open difficulties, clear up contradictions, account for dark sayings, bring to light hidden truths, in subsequent books, as you approach them in their turn, for which no mere commentator on those books will provide a substitute. And there can be little doubt that the comparatively imperfect knowledge of the Bible history which it may be feared would be found even amongst the regular attendants on our Sunday Services, would be the result of hearing the Scriptures read to them piecemeal; the chapters for the week-day Services not reaching them, and thus the continuity of the whole being disturbed and broken. But by reading the Bible through, you will see the working of God's providence gradually unfolding itself, far more distinctly than anybody can point it out to you—the dawn—the day—the perfect day. . . . You will further be led, by this practice of reading the Scriptures consecutively, to observe the several successive stages of the Gospel, considered as an integral revelation, till it attained the perfectness in which we now enjoy it. Traces of it, though only traces, in the Levitical Law; more of it disclosed in the Psalms; still more in the Prophets, and in Isaiah

That course made Christians who were well instructed in the whole Word of God. You know the book of S. Augustine, *de Catechizandis Rudibus*. You know also the *Pædagogue* of S. Clement, which is a work written for the instruction of heathens, whom he had converted in the principles of Christian philosophy. The ablest men were employed in giving those instructions, and they produced marvellous results, such as we should now consider almost beyond belief.

C: Finally, I should wish that the preacher, whoever he might be, should deliver his sermons in such a way that they would not be painful efforts to him, and that thus he would be able to preach frequently. It would be desirable that all his sermons should be short, so that he might preach every Sunday after the Gospel without inconveniencing himself, and without wearying the people.* Apparently those ancient Bishops, though

---

more especially, from whom alone it would not be difficult to extract every particular of the Gospel scheme (or nearly every particular), now that we know how to look for them."
 —J. J. BLUNT: *Duties of the Parish Priest*, pp. 76, 79.

 * "The length of the sermon oftentimes has much to do with its efficiency. That which consumes time and adds nothing to effect should be studiously avoided. Give the best thoughts in the most carefully chosen language. Study brevity. Never weary an audience. To hold a weary audience is to awaken the feeling, 'I'll not go again.' For ordinary preaching thirty or thirty-five minutes of carefully-arranged thought is more effective than more time. A certain mission preacher, after preaching an hour and a half, expressed great surprise because the

they were advanced in age, and burdened with so many labours, did not make as much difficulty as do our preachers in speaking to the people in the course of the Eucharistic Service which they were in the habit of celebrating solemnly themselves every Sunday. Nowaday, in order that a preacher may have done his duty, it seems to be thought that, when he comes from the pulpit, he should be bathed in perspiration, out of breath, and incapable of doing anything for the remainder of the day. The chasuble, which was not then cut away at the shoulders as at present, but which hung down around them equally on all sides, apparently prevented them from gesticulating as much with their arms as our preachers do. Thus their sermons were short, and their gestures grave and moderate. Is not all that, sir, according to your principles? Is not that the very idea of sermons that you give us?

---

people were not moved to decision and action. The pastor with whom he was labouring said, 'Make three sermons during the time occupied in preaching this one, and you will make three times as many converts.' Devotion ends when weariness begins."—REV. W. A. BUSHNELL.

"The good S. Francis, in his rules to the preachers of his Order, directs that their sermons should be short.

"Believe me—and I speak from experience—the more you say, the less well the hearers retain; the less you say, the more well they profit. By dint of burdening their memory you will overwhelm it; just as a lamp is extinguished by feeding it with too much oil, and plants are choked by immoderate irrigation.

"When a sermon is too long, the end effaces the middle from the memory, and the middle the beginning."—L'ABBE MULLOIS.

A: It is not mine; it is that of antiquity. The more I examine into the details of it the more I find that that ancient method of preaching was the more perfect. The men who elaborated its rules with such care, were great men; and not only of distinguished holiness, but thoroughly well acquainted with the truths of religion and the way of bringing these home to the heart and belief of men: there is wonderful wisdom hidden under their air of simplicity. We should not do well to imagine that any better method has been discovered since you, sir, have explained all that perfectly well, and have left me nothing to add: you have, in fact, developed my thought better than I could have done myself.

B: You estimate very highly the sermons and the eloquence of the Fathers.

A: I do not think I have said too much in praise of them.

B: I am surprised to see that, after having been so severe upon secular orators who have mixed *jeux d'esprit* with their speeches, you are so indulgent to the Fathers, who are full of plays upon words, antitheses and epigrams, quite contrary to all your rules. Pray reconcile these utterances of yours. For example, what do you think of the style of *Tertullian?*

A: There are very excellent sentiments in that writer: the elevation of his thought is often admirable: and it is proper to read him for the sake of historical facts, of certain principles of tradition, and for information respecting the discipline of his time. But as to his style, I do not care to defend it: he has many obscure, and even false thoughts, many harsh and entangled metaphors. But that which is faulty in him is just what the majority of readers most seek out. Many preachers are spoiled by the study of his works: they study them just because they want to say something startling. They are dazzled by the style of Tertullian, which indeed is extraordinary, and full of pomp and splendour. They ought especially to avoid imitating his style or his conceits of thought: but they may draw from his works grand ideas and considerable knowledge of antiquity.

B: And *S. Cyprian:* what do you say of him? Is he not very inflated and pompous?

A: He is so, no doubt: it is not possible to be altogether different to the fashion of one's country and one's time. But although his style and diction partake both of the inflation of his period and of African harshness, he has, nevertheless, much power and eloquence: a great and eloquent soul is everywhere visible in his writings, and he expresses his sentiments in a noble and touching manner. In some passages are to be found ornaments not in good taste; as for example in the Epistle to Donatus, which S. Augustine, nevertheless, cites[*]

De Doc. Christ. B. iv. n. 31.

as an epistle full of eloquence. That Father says that God has permitted those passages of tinsel eloquence to have escaped S. Cyprian, in order to teach posterity how greatly Christian severity has subdued in the other works of that orator the tendency to use superfluous ornament, and has brought his style within the limits of a graver and more modest eloquence. It is, says S. Augustine, that last characteristic which is marked in all the letters of S. Cyprian which follow, which may be admired without hesitation, and sought for as being in accordance with the severest rules of religion, but which cannot be equalled without much difficulty. In the main, the Epistle of S. Cyprian to Donatus, though too much ornamented, even in the judgment of S. Augustine, merits to be called eloquent: because, although you may find in it, as he says, too many flowers strewn about, you may see, nevertheless, that the bulk of the Epistle is most serious and forcible, and excellently fitted to give a high idea of Christianity to a heathen whom he desired to convert. In those passages in which S. Cyprian expresses himself with animation and earnestness, he lays down altogether those prettinesses, and takes a vehement and lofty tone.

B: But again, S. Augustine, whom you mention, is he not the very writer of all most addicted to plays upon words? Do you defend him, too?

A: I do not defend him at all in this respect. It was the fault of his time, to which his keen and acute mind rendered him more than usually prone. That shows that S. Augustine was not a perfect orator; but even with this defect, it cannot be denied that he has great power of persuasion. He is a man who reasons with singular force, who is full of noble ideas, who knows the human heart deeply and completely, who has a polished style, and is careful to observe the most exact decorum in all his discourses; and finally, who expresses himself almost invariably in a tender, loving, and winning manner. Does not such a man deserve to be forgiven for the defect which we perceive in him?

C: It is true that in him alone have I ever found one quality, that of pathos; even although he does make puns. Nothing is more filled with pathos than his *Confessions* and his *Soliloquies*. It must be confessed that they are full of tenderness, and suited to touch the feelings of the reader.

A: He corrects his tendency to play upon words, as far as that is possible, by the simplicity and directness of his transitions, and his appeals to the affections. All his works are marked unmistakably with the love of God: not only did he feel it, but he knew how to express in a marvellous way to others the feelings which he had respecting it. There he shows the tenderness which is a part of eloquence. Besides, we see that S. Augustine knew perfectly well the true rules for the preacher. He says that a discourse, in order to be persuasive, ought to be simple and natural; that art ought to be concealed; and that an excess of embellishment causes distrust in the hearer. He applies to the subject those words which you know: *He is hateful who speaks deceivingly.** He treats also, with considerable knowledge, the arrangement of subjects, the mixture of various styles, the means by which a discourse may be made to grow in a natural way, the necessity to be simple and familiar, even in the tones of the voice, as well as to use gesture at certain passages, although when speaking on a religious subject every word and gesture should be dignified: and finally, in what manner to arouse surprise and sympathy. Such are the ideas of S. Augustine respecting eloquence. But if you wish to see how completely he possessed in practice the art of putting himself in sympathy with his hearers, and of arousing their feelings, which is the true end of rhetoric, read what he himself relates respecting a discourse which he delivered to the people at Cæsarea in Mauritania, in order to abolish a barbarous practice which obtained there. It concerned an ancient custom, of which it is sufficient to say that it had been pushed to the point of monstrous cruelty. It amounted to taking away from an entire population a spectacle which delighted them: judge for yourself what was the difficulty of the enterprise. S. Augustine says that after he had spoken for some time, his hearers

---

* *De Doct. Christ.* B. ii. n. 48.

uttered cries of applause; but as long as they amused themselves with applauding him, he considered that he had not succeeded in persuading them. So that he held as of no account the pleasure and admiration of the hearers; and he only began to hope for success when he saw tears running down their cheeks. In the end, he adds, the people abandoned that spectacle, and for the last eight years it has not been renewed. Was not that a true orator? Have we any preachers at the present time who could do as much? S. Jerome, again, has his faults of style; but his expressions are masculine and noble. He has little regularity; but he is much more eloquent than most of those who pique themselves on being so. To examine the works of the Fathers, only with respect to their language and their style, would be to judge like a petty grammarian. You know well that eloquence must not be confounded with elegance and purity of diction. *S. Ambrose* also follows, sometimes, the fashion of his time: he gives to his discourse the ornaments which were then held in estimation. It may very well have been the case, perhaps, that those great men, who had views elevated above the common rules of oratory, adapted themselves to the taste of the time, in order that the Word of God might be listened to with pleasure; and in order to make for the truths of religion an entrance into hearts. But after all, do we not see S. Ambrose, notwithstanding some plays upon words, writing to Theodosius with inimitable force and persuasive power? With what tenderness does he not speak of the death of his brother Satyrus? Or we have even in the Roman Breviary a discourse from him on the head of S. John*, whom Herod respected and feared even after his death; bear it in memory, you will find the end of it sublime. S. Leo is somewhat stilted, but yet grand. Pope S. Gregory lived in an age of still worse taste; yet he has written many discourses, with much strength and dignity. It is needful to know how to distinguish in the writings of those great men, as in all other writers of their times, what is due to the bad influence of the age, from that which is to be credited to their own views, and the power of their own genius, which enabled them to influence their hearers.

C: But then, according to your view, eloquence was entirely degraded and vitiated during those ages which were so happy for religion.

A: No doubt that was the case. Soon after the Empire of Augustus, the art of eloquence and even the Latin language began, and continued to decay. The Fathers did not appear until that doctrine had begun: hence they must not be taken as faultless models in every respect; and it must even be confessed that the greater number of the sermons

---

* *De Virginibus.* B. iii. c. 6. Probably the *Decollatio S. Joannis B.*, August 29.

which were from them, are by no means their greatest works. When I was proving to you just now, by the testimony of the Fathers, that the Scripture is full of eloquence, I reflected in my own mind that they were witnesses whose own eloquence is very inferior to that which you would not believe in, except from their opinion. There are people of so depraved a taste that they are unable to feel the beauty of the prophecies of Isaiah, but who will admire S. Peter Chrysologus, in whom, notwithstanding the fine name which has been given to him, the essential qualities of Evangelical piety have to be looked for, and may be found, but under an infinity of literary faults. In the East a better style of speech and language was longer maintained, and the Greek language was preserved almost in its purity. There *S. Chrysostom* spoke it excellently: his style as you know is diffuse, but he never seeks for tawdry ornaments, and he bends all his endeavours to influence and to persuade; he arranges each subject with thought and judgment; he is well acquainted with Holy Scripture and with human character; he finds his way to the feelings he describes vividly and with power; he has just and lofty thoughts, nor is he without animation; take him for all in all, he may be called a great orator. *S. Gregory Nazianzen* is more concise and more poetical, but not sufficiently careful to persuade; he has, nevertheless, some very touching passages; for example, his farewell to Constantinople and funeral oration for S. Basil. This latter Father, again, is grave, sententious, and severe even in his diction. He had meditated deeply upon the Scripture; he was well-skilled in all human faults and errors, and of the guidance of souls he is a great master. You could hardly find anything more eloquent than his Epistle to a Virgin who had fallen; in my judgment, it is a masterpiece. Unless a correct taste is brought to the consideration of these subjects, there is a danger of choosing that which is less excellent in the Fathers, and of filling the sermons which we compose, not with their excellences, but with their faults.

C: How long did that false eloquence last, which you speak of as succeeding to the good?

A: Down to our own time.

C: Do you mean, to this very age?

A: Yes, to this very age; nor are we so far extricated from it as we suppose. You will understand the reason for this in a moment. The barbarous nations, who overspread the Roman Empire, brought everywhere ignorance and bad taste. We descend from them: and although literature began in the fifteenth century to revive, that revival has been slow. The return to the right path has been a difficult task; and there are still a great many people who do not even know what a correct taste requires. We must not cease to respect the Fathers; and not only them, but also those pious authors who have written during that long interval which separates us from them; we learn from them the tradition of the age in which they lived, and much else that is exceedingly useful and instructive. I am quite ashamed to speak in this dogmatic way; but it is, gentlemen, at your request; and please remember that I am quite ready to withdraw what I have said, if I am shown to be wrong. It is time to bring this conversation to a close.

C: But we cannot release you until you have given us your views on the manner of *choosing a text.*

A: You quite understand that the taking of texts comes from this fact: that Pastors never in earlier days, preached to the people their own personal views : they only expounded the words of the Scripture. Little by little the custom grew up of no longer following the course of the words of Scripture; only a single passage was expounded, and that was called the text of the sermon. If then an exact exposition is not made of every part of the Gospel, it is at least needful to choose words which contain the truths most important and best *fitted* to the needs of the people. Then they should be *well explained;* and in general, in order that the sense of a passage may be made quite clear, it is needful to explain many others which precede or which follow it; nor should any particularly *recondite* sense be sought for. With what bad grace does a man desire to show himself inventive and ingenious, when he ought to speak with all gravity, and with reverent regard to the authority of the Holy Spirit, whose words he borrows!

C: I confess that forced texts are always displeasing to me. Have you not remarked that a preacher draws from a text any sentiment that he pleases? He twists insensibly the subject matter, in order to fit his text to a sermon which he has to deliver. This is done especially in sermons for Lent. It is a practice I cannot approve.

B: Pray do not finish, without giving me your views on a question which has troubled me much; and after that I will not detain you.

A: Very good: let me hear what you wish. I shall be glad to do it if I can, for I greatly desire that you should employ your unquestioned ability in composing simple and persuasive sermons.

B: You wish that a preacher should expound the Scriptures consecutively, in a literal manner, according to their obvious meaning.

A: Yes; that would be most desirable.

B: How then do you account for the Fathers having done otherwise? It seems to me that their tendency is always towards *spiritual senses* of Scripture. See S. Augustine, S. Gregory, S. Bernard.* They find a mystical sense in everything,

---

* With regard to S. Bernard, his biographer, Mabillon, thus meets the charge: "It may be said, indeed, that Bernard sometimes employs

and the literal sense they do not expound at all.

A : The Jews of the time of Jesus Christ were much given to mystical and allegorical senses. It appears that the Therapeutæ, who were found principally at Alexandria, and whom Philo describes as Jewish philosophers, but whom Eusebius asserts to have been among the first Christians, were much addicted to these expositions of Scripture. It was in the same city of Alexandria that allegorical senses of Scripture began to have some currency among Christians. The first of the Fathers who diverged from the literal sense was Origen : you know the sensation that he made in the Church. At first piety inspired these interpretations ; there was something in them which was found to be at once ingenious, agreeable and edifying. Most of the Fathers, following the taste of the peoples of their time, as well as apparently, their own, made much use of them ; but they always went back faithfully to the literal sense, or to the prophetical, which is literal in its especial manner, on all subjects in

---

various texts of Scripture in a sense unfounded and far from literal, so that he seems rather to play upon the words quoted than to expound their real sense; but it is easy to reply that, there being in Scripture manifold senses, the holy man believed that he might choose that sense which seemed to him proper to edification, especially when he was not treating of any doctrine of the faith, but only proposed to himself to enlarge upon some pious thought, and thereby to attract the attention and delight of his hearers."—*Works, General Preface,* Vol. I., p. 23, *English Edition.* And the principle of the apology applies to all the other Fathers.—*Trans.*

which there was a question of setting forth the foundations of doctrine. When the people had been perfectly instructed in that which it was needful they should learn from the *letter* of Scripture, then the Fathers gave them these mystical senses to edify and to console them. These interpretations were strongly to the taste of the people, especially in the East, where they began; since they are naturally fond of mysterious and allegorical language. That variety of senses gives them extreme pleasure, as is shown by the frequent sermons and almost continuous readings from the Scriptures, which were customary in that part of the Church. But among us, where Christian people are infinitely less instructed, it is needful to give what is most necessary to them, and to commence with the literal sense, without being at all wanting in respect for those pious interpretations which have been given by the Fathers: it is needful to have bread before going to seek for *ragoûts*. With regard to the exposition of Scripture, we cannot do better than copy the sound judgment of S. Chrysostom. Most preachers in our time seek for allegorical senses, not at all because they have already sufficiently explained the literal, but to the entire exclusion of the literal, because they do not understand the greatness of it, and because they find it dry and sterile when treated in the manner in which they preach. Every part of truth and every prescription of morals is to be found in the letter of Holy Scripture; and that, not only with authority and marvellous beauty, but also with inexhaustible abundance; by associating himself with these, a preacher will have always a great number of new and great truths to bring forward, and that without recourse to mystical interpretations. It is a deplorable evil that this treasure should be so neglected, as we see it is, even by those who have it every day in their hands. If that ancient method of making homilies were adopted, there would be two classes of preachers. The one class, having neither vivacity nor poetical power would explain the Scripture simply, without adopting any specially animated or noble style. Provided that they did this in a solid and satisfactory manner, they would not fail to be excellent preachers. They would have what S. Ambrose asks for: a clear and simple style, full of weight and gravity, without affecting elegance, though not despising sweetness and acceptableness. The other class, being endowed with poetical genius, would explain the Scripture with the style and the metaphors of the Scripture itself, and thus they would become finished preachers. The one class would instruct in an effective and dignified manner; the others would add to the power of their teaching the simplicity, enthusiasm and vehemence of the Scripture: so that it will be, so to speak, entire and living in them, as much as it is possible to be in men who have not been miraculously inspired from on high.

B: Still, one moment; I forgot one important detail: but I will ask only one word of you.

A: Is there still someone else to be blamed?

B: Yes, the panegyrists. Do you not think that when the eulogy of a Saint is to be made, it is proper to depict his character, and to draw out the one special excellence of his actions and virtues?

A: That would seem as though it were chiefly intended to show the acuteness and wealth of fancy of the orator.

B: I understand you do not like that method.

A: It appears to me a false one for most of the subjects to which it may be applied. It is to do violence to facts, to try to force them all into illustrations of a single quality. There are a great number of actions in a man's life which come from various principles, and are signs of qualities very different. It is a sign of scholastic subtlety, and shows an orator who is very far from knowing human nature well, to wish to refer all actions to a single cause. The true means of making a portrait which shall be really a likeness is to depict the complete man: to put him before the eyes of the hearers, as he spoke and as he laboured. In recounting the course of his life, it is quite right to bring into the foreground those parts of it in which his natural virtues, as the graces bestowed upon him, more manifestly appear; yet something must be left for the mind and imagination of the hearer to fix upon. The best means of praising a Saint is to relate his praiseworthy actions. It is this which bestows solidity and strength to a eulogy; which instructs and impresses the hearer. Often the hearers depart without having after all a distinct idea of the life of a Saint, though they have been hearing about him for an hour: at the most, they have understood some few reflections on a small number of detached facts referred to without order. A preacher ought, on the contrary, to describe the Saint as he really existed; to show him as he was at every age, in all the conditions of his life, and at the principal conjunctures through which he passed. That would not at all prevent remarks upon his character: which would, in fact, be much better displayed by his actions and his words, than by fancy sketches and remarks.

B: You would then have the history of the Saint's life told, rather than a panegyric made upon him.

A: Pardon me, I would not make merely a simple narrative. I should content myself with making a tissue of the principal facts: but I should like that to be a concise, energetic, vigorous recital, vivid and full of animation; each word giving a lofty idea of the Saints, and serving as an exhortation to the hearer. To that I would add all such moral reflections as I thought most suitable. Do you not think that a discourse thus delivered would have a noble and attractive simplicity? Do you not think that the lives of Saints would thus be made better known, and the people more edified? Do you not even think, that according to the rules of eloquence which we have laid down, such a discourse would be more *eloquent* than all the high-flown panegyrics which one usually hears?

B: I quite see now that those sermons would be not less instructive, less touching, nor less agreeable than others. That is enough, sir; and I am quite satisfied. I feel that I ought not to detain you longer. As for me, I hope that your trouble will not be thrown away, for I am resolved to abandon the use of all the modern collections of "Extracts," and of all the Italian *Pensieri*. I mean to begin at once the study of the principles of our religion at 'first hand,' and in their sources.

C: Adieu, sir; and by way of thanks, let me assure you that I cordially agree with what you have said.

A: Adieu, gentlemen: let me take leave of you with these words of S. Jerome to Nepatian (Ep. xxxiv.): "When you shall teach in the Church, seek neither to arouse the applauses nor the groans of the people. Let the tears of your hearers be your praises. The sermon of a Priest should be full of the Holy Scripture. Do not be a mere declaimer, but a true teacher of the Mysteries of God."

www.ingramcontent.com/pod-product-compliance
Lightning Source LLC
Chambersburg PA
CBHW032146160426
43197CB00008B/789